ADVANCE PRAISE

"This book gives you ideas and strategies to select and get the job you want, get paid more and promoted faster, and fulfill your full potential at work."

BRIAN TRACY,
Author – *Goals, No Excuses!*

"The books that do the very best job of helping people reinvent their lives and careers have a magical combination of two elements: inspiration and practicality. One without the other is like a one-armed see-saw: out of balance and of very little use. Cara Heilmann's terrific book, *The Art of Finding the Job You Love*, offers the reader a generous portion of boots-on-the-ground practical information and a resonant, uplifting perspective full of possibility for the reader. If you've ever wondered why you didn't get that job or that interview, if you've puzzled over what recruiters think, if you're stuck and unsure of the path forward, this book will be an invaluable resource. Filled with practical ideas, real-life examples and fresh perspectives (Improv as a tool? Heck yes!), *The Art of Finding the Job You Love* will change the way you've been approaching your livelihood transition. It could be just what you've been needing to solve that career transition puzzle once and for all. I fully intend to recommend this book to my clients."

AMY VAN COURT, CPCC, PCC
Internationally certified career coach, speaker, and author of *Escaping Career Prison: Three Keys to Breaking Free and Finding Work You Love*

"Bam. Mic drop. Cara nailed it with her honest, helpful, and compelling book *The Art of Finding the Job You Love*. It is a must read for career coaches and anyone in career transition. I'll be recommending it (or perhaps gifting it) to my clients. I especially loved the way Cara wove the power of improv in her narrative. It may be time to dust off my improv skills and get my clients playing more!"

MARY STULTZ, MA, CPCC,
Executive Coach, Journey Of Yes

"*The Art of Finding the Job You Love* found a sweet spot—it lands between the candidate and the recruiter. Both sides would benefit from having this book in their life. This book allows the candidate to navigate towards the intent of the well-veiled questions the interviewer is throwing out. ("I am asking this, but I actually mean this.") I have interviewed tens of thousands of people across my career, I am sure. Preparation and a strategy show through when hiring, a well-thought-out approach is critical. Read this, and you are there! Many people mistake preparation for a hiring process is learning about a company—I can tell you it isn't. It is about knowing what you do and don't want, then how are you going to go about executing on that. What Cara has done here is show you how to build that roadmap."

KEVIN BLAIR,
Vice-President of Talent Acquisition, IBM

"Wow! This title says it all and Cara Heilmann delivers on all that it says! *The Art of Finding the Job You Love* is a gem for anyone who needs a modern approach on an ancient pursuit – finding the job that frees us from having to work another day in our life. But if you believe this is just another book about occupational advice, think again. Ms. Heimann's decades of experience in HR (human relationships) combine with her unique and witty perspective to provide an outside-the-cube (two dimensions cannot contain her!) view that can be applied to so many aspects of everyday life. Even if you already have the perfect position in the perfect company, her lessons can help anyone become a better employee/boss/colleague/person. Whatever your current position – leader, follower or something in between – this book will have something (or maybe everything) you need to succeed."

BYRON H. IZUKA, M.D.,
Associate Clinical Professor – University of Hawaii
Division of Orthopaedic Surgery

"Cara's many observations in working with many executives teaches you to get in touch with what you want and give yourself permission to do it differently. She highlights the career search is about more than just, giving and receiving 'facts,' it's about being yourself and connecting the dots in your life to best demonstrate who you are as a person."

CHESTER CASTILLO,
executive, consultant, and president

The Art of Finding the Job You Love

THE
ART
OF FINDING
THE JOB YOU
LOVE

AN UNCONVENTIONAL GUIDE TO WORK WITH MEANING

Cara Heilmann

NEW YORK

LONDON • NASHVILLE • MELBOURNE • VANCOUVER

The Art of Finding the Job You Love

An Unconventional Guide to Work with Meaning

Published in New York, New York, by Morgan James Publishing in partnership with Difference Press. Morgan James is a trademark of Morgan James, LLC. www.MorganJamesPublishing.com

The Morgan James Speakers Group can bring authors to your live event. For more information or to book an event visit The Morgan James Speakers Group at www.TheMorganJamesSpeakersGroup.com.

ISBN 9781683509912 paperback
ISBN 9781683509929 eBook
Library of Congress Control Number: 2018934766

Cover Design by:
Christopher Kirk
www.GFSstudio.com

Interior Design by:
Chris Treccani
www.3dogcreative.net

In an effort to support local communities, raise awareness and funds, Morgan James Publishing donates a percentage of all book sales for the life of each book to Habitat for Humanity Peninsula and Greater Williamsburg.

Get involved today! Visit
www.MorganJamesBuilds.com

To Dad.
Thank you for loving me without judgment.

To Mom.
Thank you for believing I can be anything I want to be.

WARNING

This book contains unconventional ideas, tips, and advice—uncommon and, some would say, off-the-wall. If you are looking for guidance that you've read and heard for the past 20 years—a refresher course or a rehash—close this book now. Return it immediately. This book is not for you. But if you are looking for ideas that are fresh and could provide the edge you are needing, read on. The tips in this book have been known to cause clarity, confidence, and enthusiasm in your journey to finding work you love.

TABLE OF CONTENTS

INTRODUCTION

Think off-center.
– GEORGE CARLIN

I'm not funny. What I am is brave.
– LUCILLE BALL

Daniel and I were sitting at Geppetto's Cafe in Orinda when he said something that captured what many others before him have said: "There's so much information out there. I am just not sure how much of this *job search thing* I want to learn about." Here he is after 30 years into his career, learning a completely new thing—one that he hasn't had to deal with in a long time and that he's never had to learn much about in all his working years: finding a job. But, unlike his first job out of college, he's wiser and assured of his direction. Now, he doesn't want just any job. He wants to do something with meaning. Something a little bit righteous. One that makes him happy, allows him to give back, and lights a fire in his soul. But something is amiss in his job search process—after 30 years of leading teams, he keeps coming in second place in the interview process and he doesn't know why.

I identify with Daniel. Maybe you do, too. For the past 20 years, you and I have sat on opposite sides of the negotiating table. I've interviewed hundreds of you and even fallen in love with you thinking you would be the perfect person for the team. But for one reason or another, the organization decided to focus on another person. I've read your emails asking for feedback on why you didn't get a job offer. I've wanted to share ideas and tips. I knew my boundaries as a representative of the company, but yearned to share information that would be valuable to you. I've heard in your voice exasperation about the length of a process, about needing to come back once more to interview with someone else. I could tell that it was a frustrating process for you. Maybe even demoralizing.

The job search process is a roller coaster ride of highs and lows. One moment the recruiter is all over you and very interested in your skills. The next, you can't get them to reply to your email. Someone said, "It feels like I'm dating again!" A lot of unknowns. Filled with insecurities and questions like, "Does she like me? Why hasn't he called?" It's enough to chip away at the confidence of even incredibly successful people.

You are a doer—the person who gets things done. You solve problems. You make amazing deals. You inspire people and build communities. You've had a career full of achievements and proud moments. Through your style, passion, and grit, you've made incredible differences in the lives of companies, your teams, and customers. I love hearing your accomplishments.

Sometimes my mouth is hanging on the floor listening to the amazing things you've done. Yet, for many, the job search process feels like one big fail. The job search landscape has changed since the last time you've looked for a new job. There is a lot to learn. Where do you start?

Do you remember when we'd send our résumé and cover letter via snail mail? Now we have applicant tracking systems that make the process much easier for the recruiter; however, it takes you 45 minutes just to upload a résumé only to get an instant rejection email. Why? You conduct a search and learn that if you don't have the right keywords in your résumé, the applicant tracking system will reject your candidacy. For the few that do not result in an automatic system rejection, you receive an email a few days later that says, *"Thank you so much for your application. We've reviewed your application and have regretfully decided to focus on another candidate. We'll keep your application on file..."* Painful, but better than the more common response of silence.

It's a company's market—unemployment is such that there are significantly more candidates for each open position these days. Long ago, when I was recruiting for an Executive Assistant, I posted the job and received over 1,500 résumés in two days. I had to take the posting down or else I'd spend the next few days sifting through these résumés. How does anyone shine in a competitive market like the one we have today? Things are automated. Companies are reducing the number of recruiters because of the automation. Thus each recruiter has more open positions to fill. Recruiters are going at 100 mph to keep up with more open positions, calls from hiring managers who need a position filled right away, and an overabundance of candidates for each vacancy. Because of this, recruiters seek round pegs to fill round holes—it is easier to fill a role with someone who was doing the same thing for a competitor. But, what if you, like Daniel, have the experience to do the job, but you don't look like it on paper? The titles are just a little off or the industry is not perfectly aligned. How will recruiters see that you can do the job?

Daniel was making a career pivot after 30 years as a rabbi. Instead of teaching young adults about faith and community through a bar or bat mitzvah preparation, he wanted to work with adolescents who are seeking faith and a community to plug into. Daniel spoke to and met with many nonprofits throughout the area that serve this niche. At the writing of this book, Daniel is in the interview process with several companies, so perhaps by the time we're finished writing, we'll know if he landed the job. Like many others, Daniel is making a slight career pivot—a direction that is very much in alignment with his experience and passion. Yet organizations are struggling with his previous titles and not seeing how what he did for his congregation is exactly what they are seeking.

I wrote this book for you. You've had a full and amazing career. Now you want to do something a little different. As one executive said, "After 20 years in retail, I want to do something virtuous and give back somehow." And like Daniel, you may be struggling with just how to articulate all that you've done in the job search process. I've been on the other side for many years, working as a recruiter. I have heard stories by candidates who are making a similar pivot. I've heard compelling stories that made sense, and other stories that didn't. I want to give you a peek behind the curtain of recruiting to shed light on what may be going on at the organization. To explain what recruiters and organizations are looking for. The answers they want to hear.

It's not what you think. It isn't a silver bullet of the perfect response that will land you any job. Recruiters and hiring managers want to get to know the real you during the interview process. And if you get the job, they'll see the real you in a few months anyway. They want to decide whether the real you would be a contributing, valuable member of their team, and they want to make that decision before you start. They want to know if your personality would fit in their world. They want to know if you'll be one of the top hires.

On the flip side, you're selective as well. You're no longer going to just accept any offer that comes your way. It needs to be a great fit for you and for them.

This book outlines tips of how you can show up as the real you.

There is something very attractive about someone who is self-confident. You've seen this person. They walk into the room and it's like the sun has entered with them. They carry this sense of charisma and approachability so strong that you just want to turn and smile and say, "Hey!" I might even be describing you. I call it charisma—some call it a "great aura." Whatever it's called, it's the ability to connect with another human being and be self-assured, without concern over whether they like you. You're excited to meet them and to get to know them. I believe we can teach people to turn up the volume of this thing, this charisma. I believe we can teach people to increase their aura, their thing, so that people are drawn to you during the job search process. And I believe the way to do this is to turn up the volume of the real you, the thing that employers want to know.

CHAPTER 1

Should I Stay or Should I Go?

I'll try anything once, twice if I like it,
three times to make sure.
— MAE WEST

In economics, there is a term called *barriers to exit* that refers to the many hurdles to leave a market, sector, or offering. A company with a dying product is considering discontinuing the line; but the cost to do so is prohibitive. A termination fee is a barrier to exit. It will cost you money to end a contract–make it more painful to leave than to stay. Sometimes barriers to exit are so high that the barrier outweighs the potential gain from moving on. I faced a big barrier to exit in my career.

In college, I picked the major that I thought would get me closest to what my mom was–an amazing person and leader, surrounded by people who respected her and worked for her over long periods of time. The closest thing at my college was human resources. Recruiting, leadership, retention. It sounded great. It was a major in *people*, right? It didn't take long for that dream to turn dark.

Two years after graduating, I was telling a guy who had been with the company for 35 years that his job was gone. We were closing the plant. Shutting the entire operation down. Slimming down to get the rest ready for sale. We were all going to be let go. The leadership team had talked about the possibility for weeks, yet this guy was shocked. He was angry. He was mad at the company. He was mad at the leaders. He was mad at the venture capitalist company that was trying to sell us. And he focused all his anger on me–the closest person to him telling him news that he dreaded hearing. He screamed at me. He pounded his fists on the table. I thought he was going to jump across the table and attack me. Chris, who worked in the next office came in to help the employee leave. After they left, I looked down at my list and scanned the names of the remaining 24 people I had to repeat that process with. It wasn't a good day for me. It wasn't a good day for people in general. Not a great example of why I got into human resources. Yet, even after that, I stayed in the field.

I climbed the ladder. I got my first manager position. Then a regional role. Soon I was leading the HR function for large divisions of key sectors of the business. I managed more terminations, employee relations nightmares, downsizing, rightsizing, and lawsuits. I stayed in a field that I didn't really love because I felt like I couldn't leave. I had a bachelor's degree in HR and a master's degree in HR and, by that time, 20 years in the field. The thought of leaving this expertise was a massive barrier to exit. So, I got good at mixing it up.

To break the monotony of the job, I changed companies at a regular clip. To stay for four years at one location was a long tenure. I had to keep moving to refresh my reserves, or else the drain on my emotional bank would begin to sap me. Because I had a knack at writing my own résumé and preparing for interviews, I'd land a new job with ease. I just wouldn't stay very long. I found areas that I loved at the fringe of HR and would pour my heart into them, like being on a national diversity council or stabilizing a market for an HR consulting firm. No one could tell that I wasn't happy. Then I worked for a boss who could tell.

My boss was an incredible public figure in international circles. He was charismatic. Magnetic. He had an amazing capacity to move crowds of people as a keynote speaker. And he liked to have people around him that were devoted to him. I thought he was a great public figure, but I wasn't a devotee. It wasn't his fault. I'm a low-hierarchy organization, slightly irreverent kind of person. My lack of devotion didn't float his boat. After too many inadvertent leaks of my neutrality (that he read as disrespect), he asked me to leave. I was the second person on his executive team that he let go. After I left, he let go a third. Before I left, other leaders in the organization offered roles in other departments, yet I couldn't shake the idea that a weight had been lifted from me. It wasn't the company.

It wasn't my boss. It wasn't even the field of HR. It was the need to do *my thing*–I had a calling. It wasn't compliance or issuing written warnings. I had to find My Thing.

I combined everything I loved about my job and founded a coaching business to help people find jobs they love. Every day doing that work felt great. It was like a breath of fresh air. I fell in love with every person I worked with. I helped hundreds of people find amazing jobs. But that's not the end of the story. This is where it gets crazy.

In the middle of all of this, I was asked to be Chief Talent Officer at a Silicon Valley startup. The founder was amazing, and she was onto something big! It wouldn't be all HR, she said. What did I do? I took the job and jumped right back into the muck again. But, unlike other slow creeps, my "yuck" reaction was immediate. Gone were the conversations with my job-seeking clients. Goodbye to career strategy sessions. I had fallen off my island. Yet I told myself to hang on. The stocks were coming. This was going to be big. BIG! Then I could go back to what I was doing. I'd say this to myself every single miserable day.

Then something terrible happened. Something that rocked my world. I lost my dad. What he thought was gall stones turned out to be liver disease. Before they could operate on him, he caught pneumonia and died. Through his passing, I found my way back again. Back to my island where I belong and where I need to stay because life is too darned short. It is too short to be mucking around in the yuck.

I share this story with you because, if you feel like you've hit a career U-turn, I want you to know that you are not alone.

Perhaps another job that started out great is slowly turning into a dread. You crave using all your talents, all of your skills. And it just feels like you've stagnated in a role that didn't grow with you. You feel like it's time for something different. To find your island. Your Thing.

This is not a book that will help you create a résumé. It is not a book that will help you update your LinkedIn profile. This book is about the moment where the rubber meets the road in the job search process. The moment when a recruiter calls you. The moment you speak to the hiring manager. The moment when you need to connect with another person in the job search process.

I'm so excited to share these ideas with you. It's your time. I'm honored that I may have a small part in your journey to finding a job you love.

CHAPTER 2

If I'm So Smart, Why Is This Hard?

*Sometimes you can't see yourself clearly until you see
yourself through the eyes of others.*
— ELLEN DEGENERES

F inding a job isn't new territory. You've been on this
ride before. You know the routine, and in fact, you may
have sat on the other side of the table. Perhaps you've
interviewed many people over the years and know what you
like to hear in the interview. Yet today it feels just a little
bit different. Like you've entered a parallel universe where
everything looks a little sharper and the ground is a little
tilted. And in many ways, you have.

At first glance, it may look the same. Getting a job is
something you've done many times in the past. Take my

client Ken, for instance. He not only has been hired many times over his incredibly successful 20-year career, he and his team have made thousands of employment offers as a Global Talent Acquisition team. You'd think Ken would be a pro at getting a job. But, in some strange way, his experience actually made it a bit harder. Because he knew so much, this job search process felt too familiar.

Howard, on the other hand, wasn't at all familiar with the job search process. A new graduate fresh out of school with a few internships under his belt, Howard was preparing for an in-person interview with a company for a Data Analyst. The week prior we talked about how to prepare for interview questions. We recently had his mock interview. He completely nailed it. I asked him if he had practiced and he said that he did, hundreds of times in front of a mirror and then had three of his friend interview him. I was astonished. Not knowing what to expect, Howard went the extra mile to prepare. But for Ken, with 20 years' experience of interviewing others, the interview set-up is all too familiar. "I'll just wing it," was Ken's response to interview prep. In my experience, people who are successful tend to approach the job search process too casually.

Success. It's a double-edged sword. The more you've done, the more achievements you've had, the experience of high-visibility roles, the harder it is to narrow down how you can help another company. Which thing do you pick to talk about? Howard has two internships' worth of work experience. You? You may have 25+ years of multiple successes. Preparing for the interview might be harder for the accomplished and successful.

YOU'VE DONE A LOT AND BECAUSE OF THAT, YOU CAN DO A LOT

More About Ken

I first met Ken at a small cafe on a beautiful day with a green golf course as our backdrop. He showed me his résumé. He was the global head of talent acquisition for a major tech firm in the Bay Area. He led a large team of 150 employees scattered across Asia, Europe, and South America with an impressive list of achievements. Before that, he worked for another massive tech firm leading international talent acquisition. His résumé was a list of the best top tech firms in the world leading global talent acquisition. "So, what's next for you? You can go anywhere with your background," I asked Ken. "That is exactly my struggle," sighed Ken. "I could work for another tech firm or a small start-up or outside of tech. I'm having a hard time articulating exactly what I want to do now." I've seen this before. The more you've done, the greater the list of achievements and successes in your past, the harder it is to articulate what you can contribute during a job search process.

YOUR PREVIOUS JOB TITLES DON'T DESCRIBE YOUR NEXT MOVE

Remember Daniel? Daniel worked for 30 years as a rabbi. He was ready to make a pivot in his career to be a shepherd of a community nonprofit instead of a congregation. He led very large congregations and has grown very small congregations, all the while earning multiple community awards. As he faced this pivot in his career, he struggled to articulate his move. "People ask me, 'so, what do you want to do now?' And I sound wishy-washy," he told me. Like Ken, he can do many things. He has coordinated widely connected inter-faith efforts to bring tolerance and inclusion to thousands of people over the years. His ability to build coalitions and create a vision of purpose is truly a valuable talent. And he could do the same for a host of other causes. "I need an elevator pitch that captures 30 years of success in 60 seconds or less," he said.

Do You Have the Wrong Job Title?

After you've been successful at a company for many years, leaders have recognized your talents and added on more to your plate. You've enthusiastically accepted the additional tasks and taken projects to the next level. Over the years, you've found joy in these side tasks. But it can be difficult to tell recruiters about these roles and the skills you've gained from them when your job title has been something completely different. My client Pamela, for example, has had a lifetime of experience working for the city as a Computing Systems Manager. In addition to her full-time job, for the past 20 years she'd been tasked with putting together events—

from small VIP intimate affairs to large events for thousands of people. Pamela was always in the middle of every event, making it flow as perfectly as possible. If the caterer was late, Pamela was on it. The entertainment forgot a major piece of AV equipment? Don't fret, Pamela was there to save the day. Pamela seamlessly addressed these issues with grace and ease. So when she was hunting for a new job, she wanted to apply for an Event Planning Manager position. Unfortunately, though, none of her job titles reflected this skill. Despite numerous attempts, recruiters bypassed her qualifications because her title didn't fit. It was only through connections, she was able to talk with a recruiter. Then she was able to tell a story of how she was meant to contribute to an organization as a full-time event planner. In Pamela's situation, she knew her next career move. But some people can't see their successes because what they did, not matter how amazing, was just part of the job.

TO YOU, AMAZING IS (YAWN) NORMAL

Manuel Couldn't See His Success

After 15 years in the US Army, Manuel decided to leave and make the jump to civilian life. He struggled to find a career direction. I asked him to share some of his successes over his long career with the military. "I just followed orders. Everything I did was because I was told to do so by my commanding officer," said Manuel. I approached his achievements from a different angle. I asked, "Was there anything that you've done that you were proud of? Even if it was something you were ordered to do?" That's when Manuel told me of a doozy of a story.

"I was deployed and asked by my C.O. to set up a medical facility for a military prison. With a degree in nursing and direct medical care experience, I met with others to understand the number of prisoners we would hold at this facility. The number of military personnel. The number of contractors. I estimated the types of ailments and set out to establish this medical facility. I ordered all the supplies and personnel needed to staff the medical facility. And within six months we had a fully operational hospital."

I was stunned. "Do you realize how incredible this is?" I asked Manuel. "COOs of major hospitals do not have this depth and breadth of experience."

He replied, "I was just following orders."

Although Manuel was proud of this event, he didn't see it as an achievement as it was all part of what he was told to do. From this success and others that he reluctantly shared, Manuel realized that what he loved to do and had a talent for was leading complex projects within a healthcare environment. He found a job as a Project Manager for a major hospital system in his hometown. With the different titles and nomenclature of the military, it wasn't obvious that to him that he should focus on Project Management.

THINGS HAVE CHANGED SINCE THE LAST TIME YOU LOOKED FOR A JOB

Companies Are Tech-Dependent

Gone are the days of sending your résumé and cover letter to the hiring manager. I'm not even talking about snail mail–I'm talking about *email*. With the lowered cost of applicant tracking systems (ATS), every organization–both big and small–can implement one. Because of that, the ATS has become the primary tool for candidates to introduce themselves to organizations. Today, you upload your document to the ATS and it extracts information from your résumé into the database. It tracks and manages all communication and interfaces with email. It automatically posts jobs to multiple online job boards. Now people from across the nation, or even world, can apply for a position with a few clicks. You are now competing against talented people from all across the globe.

There Are a Lot of Candidates Looking for Jobs

It is common for a recruiter to post a position on a Friday and take it down on a Monday because of the high number of people that applied for the job over the weekend. Job aggregators that comb through the internet looking for jobs to post on their own website make it very easy for candidates from all over to find and apply to jobs. For example, Indeed. com is one of the largest and most popular job search engines today. Remember the Executive Assistant position that I mentioned in the introduction? The one where I received 1,500 résumés in two days? I wasn't as concerned about the volumes of résumés because I added questions to the ATS application process. These five questions were required for all candidates to answer and were the minimum requirements of the job. By glancing at my ATS dashboard, I was able to see which candidates met the minimum qualifications of the job. I had also added two stretch qualifications–higher education and direct industry experience–that identified the much smaller set of candidates that exceeded the minimum qualifications. I was able to reduce 1,500 candidates to 200 that met the minimum qualifications, and further down to 70 that exceeded the qualifications. It was those 70 whose résumés I actually opened. Without the power of the ATS, I would've been reading through stacks of résumés for several days. There are a lot of candidates vying for a few positions. If you are one of the few that are still in the running, how do you stand out?

Having a lot of experience under your belt makes it harder to clearly articulate your direction. And having a lot of success might give you a sense of comfort that you could wing it. We are going to use your experience and success to your advantage. We're going to leverage your smarts, your grit, your experience, and your record of achievement. We're going to use these things to help you stand out from the pack using a process that is avant-garde. It is outside of conventional wisdom and a fresh approach to the age-old interview process.

I'm going to share a unique way to prepare for the job search process. This way incorporates a fun, fresh, and radically different way to help you get a job that you love. Whether you're three or thirty years in the workforce, this system can help you refine and articulate your wide array of skills so that you come across exactly as you intend: perfectly suited for their role. This new approach uses the same techniques taught in improv comedy. "Wait, did you just say improv? Or did you mean *improve*?" Yes, I said improv. Stay with me for a bit. Similar to improv, job interviews require you to quickly pull answers out of thin air. You are speaking with a recruiter and you need to present information on the spot. And just like in improv, nothing is more frustrating than freezing up in an interview.

What you may not know is that improv comedians spend time preparing. It just appears very spontaneous. These techniques taught in improv will help you turn your achievements into compelling stories that leave your audience wanting more. Clamoring for more of you. Anxious to get you on their teams. And, the preparation doesn't need to be boring. It can actually be fun.

A small warning, though: These improv techniques and games are going to feel strange. You might feel a bit silly—and that is the point. Because in improv we're supposed to laugh. The process of trying something new, stretching beyond our comfort zones, falling on our faces, and laughing at ourselves are all part of it. Laughing at ourselves is exactly what we should be doing when we play improv games.

So let's give it a shot. Let's do a bit of improv together.

CHAPTER 3

Combat the Success Trap: Prepare Like the Pros

You have to go through the falling down in order to learn to walk. It helps to know that you can survive it. That's an education in itself.
– CAROL BURNETT

I n this chapter, we are integrating the world of improv with the interview process. We'll discuss the parts of improv that we would like to weave into our preparation process and see how real job seekers have used these improv techniques to help them land jobs they love.

INTROVERTS FIND VALUE IN IMPROV

Amit received two to three calls a week from recruiters. There was something about Amit's online profile that drew recruiters to him. His fluency in a string of programming languages and a profile photo that made him look like the most easy-going team player. Like clockwork, his cellphone would ping and let Amit know that another recruiter had reached out to him. After several months of talking with recruiters, Amit began to worry that his dream of working for a high-tech company in Silicon Valley would never materialize. Of the many recruiters he had talked to, not one invited him to continue with the interview process.

The problem? Amit was incredibly introverted—not unlike other brilliant programmers. His love was solving problems through code, not conversations. He struggled with the telephone conversations with recruiters. He would get tongue-tied. He'd second guess what he had just said and struggled to sound confident. Together we played a few improv games and his confidence rose. We'd start our coaching session with a short improv game that could be done over video conference. I'd start a sentence and Amit would need to finish it. Then I'd say a complete thought and Amit would need to add on to the idea. We laughed together, and Amit's skill at thinking quickly on his feet improved. Amit received two job offers. Today Amit is a programmer at Netflix, with gobs of RSU stocks worth gobs of money.

WHY IMPROV WORKS IN INTERVIEW PREP

Improv games create a safe space to practice thinking on our feet. This safe space is a perfect environment for introverts like Amit to experiment. At my first improv class at the Berkeley Improv, they put us on stage. And in almost every class after that we went on stage. By the time the weeks were over, the stage held little fear for me. The stage became just a place. In each class, we'd play different improv games. At first, I couldn't tell what we were learning. But as the weeks went by, the purpose became clear. I began to have greater awareness and control over three things: my body, my voice, and my persona. I learned to give up over-thinking. Thinking about a response ahead of time was futile. When it was my turn, I learned to say the first thing that came to my mind. I learned to listen: to the group, to my partner, to myself. I learned to expand on what my partner had just said, and make an opening for more material. I experienced the power of words that would open a door on creativity. I learned what it meant to play to the *top of my intelligence*. Through my play with improv at this group and others, I began to see how these concepts could help many people express themselves exactly as they wanted to. To come across as their real, authentic self who is experienced, successful, and brilliant.

IMPROV LESSONS THAT GET YOU TO THE TOP OF YOUR GAME

In improv and comedy in general, there is a challenge to play or perform to the top of your intelligence. You've seen this. Watching a comedian say something so brilliant that you would laugh for days after thinking about it. The funniest improv is when someone says something *brilliant*. In comedy, it is considered the easy way to say something that would get a cheap laugh. When you stretch high or dig deep and something pops out that is utterly, brilliantly funny, that is when you are playing to the top of your intelligence. Robin Williams was a brilliant comedian. So quick, so funny. He is an excellent example of a comedian playing to the top of his intelligence.

Let's be clear. I am not suggesting you try to be hilarious during interviews. It is the brilliant response that is exactly what we want to do in an interview—play to the top of our intelligence.

IMPROV LESSONS THAT BRING AWARENESS TO HOW YOU CARRY YOURSELF

Throughout the classes, something else started to happen as well. Perhaps it was the constant process of standing on stage—learning to control my body by using it to tell a story and support the character I was playing—I started to *feel* more confident. I started to feel full, big, expansive. What was going on? Researchers call this *embodied cognition,* where there is a direct link between your body posture and your mood. Feeling sad? It may be because you're sitting slumped in a chair or curled up on your bed. Maybe it's your mood that is affecting your body? Research indicates that it could also go the other direction: Your body position is fueling your feelings. This would support my experience with body control through my practice with improv. I felt more confident, fuller, bigger, and more expansive. This is exactly how we should show up at an interview.

IMPROV HELPS YOU USE YOUR VOICE TO TELL STORIES

Long ago, I took voice lessons. In each lesson, my teacher would take my voice through a series of sounds during our warm-up. Improv does something similar. Through the portrayal of different characters, you stretch your vocal range. You morph between being an annoying nasally sniveling child, to a giant tromping through the woods, to the quiet voice of a spider spinning a web in a corner. Improv allows you to practice and stretch your voice as you master these different voices to support your character. Through this vocalization, I've become aware of how I sound and how I come across, gaining greater control over how I present myself. This voice awareness and control helps you connect over the telephone and also use your voice to tell your career stories.

IMPROV HELPS YOU CONNECT WITH THE RECRUITER

As a recruiter, I'd tell candidates this: "I know you can do the job based on everything on your résumé and previous interviews. Today, we want to get to know you to see if you'd have good chemistry with our team." Chemistry. Connection. This is what hiring leaders want to determine in an interview. They are asking, "Can I work with this person?" and, "Will I enjoy working with this person?" Dale Carnegie's book *How to Win Friends and Influence People* speaks to this subject. Pair this with the charisma that improv develops, and you will have a very powerful combination in your job search process.

IMPROV TAUGHT ME THE IMPORTANCE OF PREPARATION

In Steve Martin's comedy Masterclass course, one of the first lessons with budding comedians is talking about their written skits. He has read through the skits and pulled out different stories to discuss and use in the course. Which stories are powerful. Which could be unique and brilliant. Which need more help. Together, the students pick and poke apart each one to see how, with Steve's coaching, the comedian could use the material and turn it into something funny.

This lesson highlights how successful comedians are prepared. Although it appears as though a comedian is talking off the cuff, it is probably the work of hours of preparation. How many of us write out our interview stories? I'd say the typical job seeker practices speaking their answers. However, how many actually write out the stories? One thing I've learned from improv is that something creative happens when we write out our stories.

IMPROV COMBINED WITH YOUR STORIES OF SUCCESS

In each class my timing improved, my body pushed my emotions, and my voice became more intentional. I thought I was getting better at being bold. However, what I realized was that I was becoming more *aware*. More aware of how my words and movement fed into another scene…or didn't. How my responses opened the door for my partner to run with a funny idea. How if I stayed away from over-thinking, my immediate responses were actually funnier. It is impossible to think "what if?" in improv because the scene changes so quickly. Improv teaches you how to stay present–right here, right now. I found my voice. With no time to pretend, my true, raw, authentic self materialized on stage. And she was big, bold, and funny as heck. I discovered my own voice. Powerful, intentional, and clear.

After years and years of helping people prepare for interviews, improv has been a game changer for me. It has created a safe space for professionals, successful business people, famous community leaders, executives, physicians, and the like to try something different. To practice skills that help us bring out our true voice. To combine the body and voice control with our stories–written, edited, and rehearsed. So that when a question is thrown at us, we respond immediately, with confidence, and in a compelling way. Now that I've enticed you to practice with improv, let us continue to take steps to find a job with meaning. The journey starts with getting very clear on your ideal job. I'll share steps that have helped hundreds of people find a job they love. It starts with one job and by pinpointing your focus, you open your world. Let's do this!

CHAPTER 4

Focus on One Job, Become Attractive to Many

The other trick I use when I have a momentary stoppage…go to an already published novel and find a sentence that you absolutely adore. Copy it down…that will lead you to another sentence and pretty soon your own ideas will start to flow.
— STEVE MARTIN

During an informational interview, the community leader asked Daniel, "What do you want to do?" "I was stumped!" said Daniel. "That's the thing, I can do community work with the homeless, with feeding the hungry, with inter-faith events, with working with the youth, with ending poverty. There is so much I can do." "But, what do you, deep down in your heart, want to do?" I asked.

You can do a lot. You have so many talents and skills that you've accumulated over the years. You have experience and wisdom and could apply these things to many different jobs. But recruiters don't have the time to see all those things. They are looking for obvious clues that you can do exactly what they are seeking. The more you sound like a generalist, the more you don't sound like their solution. But take a tip from marketing, where experts say to identify a narrow niche and attract customers based on that one thing—then expand once they're loyal followers.

There is an overall hesitancy to get narrow. Job seekers feel that if they go too narrow, they'll miss other potential opportunities. They'll inadvertently say "no" to things that they could do. Better to cast a wider net to catch more fish, goes the logic. I understand this line of thinking. And yet I know from experience that the opposite happens. When you narrow down your ideal job, you become much more attractive to employers.

WHERE INTELLIGENCE MEETS PASSION

Kathy was brilliant. I could tell from the first conversation. She was exceptionally smart. She had a degree from Northwestern in neuroscience. She's worked with famous researchers made sense of trillions of pieces of information. She's applied her talents to medical writing while working with pharmaceutical companies attempting to get a new drug through the rigorous FDA process. She asked me to help her prepare for a medical writing job. But when she spoke about medical writing, she sounded tired and dispirited. I could hear it in her voice. "Kathy, what do you really want to do?" I asked her.

After she talked a bit about how medical writing is a challenge and that she loves challenges, she told me that deep down, she wants to be part of a team that creates a medical device that grants access to thousands who could never get access. People who live in the remotest areas of the world who could never get care without this device.

Could Kathy be an exceptionally competent and successful medical writer? You bet. She could have many successful years in the field moving up the career ladder and eventually teaching junior medical writers about the nuances of writing for a certain protocol. But should she?

You can do a lot in this world. You have capabilities that can help your career move far and fast. You are smart and capable. But in the end, it is important to narrow down the job search to just one job. This process can help you better express yourself to a wider audience.

WHY IT IS IMPORTANT TO NARROW YOUR FOCUS

Something happens in our brains when we set a goal of our ideal job. Once we identify a target, we begin to move in that direction. Brian Tracy, the guru of getting things done (this is my term for him), has talked about this phenomenon in all his 30+ books including my favorites, *Maximum Achievement* and *Eat That Frog!* There is power in setting a goal and the more specific you can be, the more powerful.

It is as if the entire universe begins to converge to move you in that direction. Let us leverage that momentum in the job search process.

HOW DO I REFINE MY TARGET?

Go online and search for your ideal job. It might be in a location you would not want to relocate to; however, find that job that makes your soul swoon. I've seen ideal jobs from SpaceX to Zappos to the company down the street. Clients are excited about the opportunity. If landed, it would be an exciting role. The job must be one which you have the minimum qualifications to do, right now. It is from that ideal job that everything flows...from the résumé, the cover letter, the LinkedIn profile, to the stories that you'll create. You may not end up working there. But it gives you a target. A finite mark to shoot for. A bullseye to hit. It is usually at this point in the process that something comes into the picture. Something that has the best of intentions but that, somehow, ends up sabotaging us along the way: our amygdala.

MEET YOUR AMYGDALA: FRIEND OR FOE?

Once you set your eyes on the prize of your ideal job, your amygdala goes into high gear to keep you safe—and while it is keeping you safe, it keeps you small. The amygdala is a small almond shaped part of your brain that has many useful (and some not very useful) functions. When you were young, your amygdala warned you when you were about to run across a busy street. "Hey, don't go there, remember mommy said to always hold an adult's hand." It is also the warning signal that raises suspicions when entering a space that might be dangerous for you. However, it can go in overdrive and warn you about things that do not need any warning at all. And because of this, your amygdala can help to keep you small (as it tries to keep you safe).

You'll begin to hear your amygdala say many things that sounds like this, "You should just get another medical writing job. It will be easier." Just fall back to what you've always done. It's safer. Don't step out and reach for the stars. The bigger they are, the harder they fall. You will get rejected. "Remember when you were in high school and you tried to get that award? And you stood on stage with the other two finalists and she got the prize and not you?" (This is one of my amygdala's favorite recollections of a very public failure. This and falling right in front of my crush in middle school.)

Your amygdala will try very hard to keep you safe. There are many other times your amygdala will come into the picture. It is helpful to recognize when your amygdala is trying to "help" you. Often it starts to become louder when you think up your ideal job. You are stepping into something big, and to your amygdala, big is scary. My recommendation is to quiet the amygdala and push through this process (tips to help mentioned later in the book).

WHAT IF I AM STUCK DOING SOMETHING I DON'T LIKE?

What if you know you need to make a pretty big career pivot? It may be a nagging feeling or an inkling that you aren't in the right role. If that is the case, I recommend you spend a bit of time thinking of and reflecting on the new direction you should take. It might not be the job of your dreams. But your next move might be a step in the right direction. Let me introduce you to someone who, after a lifetime working in his family's business, was ready to make a pretty radical pivot in his career.

Alex learned almost every part of the company's operations. The plan was for him to continue in the family business and possibly take over one day. But something changed in his heart during his master's degree studies of organization design—all his beliefs about how to move things forward in a radical way now had names attached to them: change management, transformational change, cultural integration. He knew there was something else for him to do. But he didn't know exactly what that might be. Let me share the process we took to help Alex uncover his next steps.

Together we looked back at Alex's life, from birth until the present moment, talking about times in his life that he felt completely alive, successful, happy. He shared about places he lived, friends he made, places he visited. In the end, we captured several themes around family, mentorship, challenging times, self-dependence, authenticity, and his unique way of seeing things differently.

He shared about times in his current work that he felt alive and fulfilled. As I listened to his story, I wrote down themes—overcoming a massive challenge, feeling bored when things turn to maintenance mode, building something from nothing, and walking the operations floor connecting with employees.

I asked him to tell me what he would put on a billboard if thousands of people could see it. He said, "Be Your True Self."

I asked him for the approximate amount of money he would like to earn–knowing that this career pivot might involve a salary cut. This is important. Because from what he said, he could be a great corporate trainer; however, based on the salary he said he wanted, he would never consider the role. From all that he said, I began to describe three different roles that he might really enjoy.

The first was with Blommer's Chocolates, which was looking for an Operations Director. After speaking with the Chief HR Officer on the East Coast, we learned that this family-owned and run business was seeking someone who could work independently from the mothership and who would take this 1,000-employee chocolate manufacturing plant and make transformational changes to its infrastructure and operations.

Alex was surprised by this option, as it wasn't one that he had considered in the past. There were things that were familiar and things that were new and challenging with this opportunity. It was a potential.

The second option was ARAMARK, which was looking for a Director of Business Development to search for opportunities within the existing client base and outside. It involved collaborating with regional leaders to identify ways to expand the business and making presentations to clients. He would also have to seek out new sales opportunities by building relationships with potential clients and creating sales presentations with operations leaders. And then once the business was sold, the job would transition into working alongside the operations team for a period to ensure execution as the client expected.

Alex really liked this second option because he loved sales and would love to collaborate with operations to meet client expectations. This would be a greater stretch for him than the Bloomer's Chocolates position.

The third option was with the Hay Group. This group was looking for Consultants to partner with executives who wanted transformational change within their work environments. Someone else may be involved in selling and closing the deal, but Alex would be part of the sales process. Once the deal was closed, he would be part of a team that would go into the organization and assess the current state of affairs. Then he would work closely with the team and company executives to craft a plan forward to address the company's problems.

After I mentioned the Hay option, Alex was silent on the phone for a while. Then he said, almost in a whisper, "This is exactly what I want to do." He loved the idea of helping as many companies as he could—not just one, but many. He also loved the idea of getting in deep with different organizations; speaking with employees, learning about the ins and outs, and coming back with a top-level strategic plan with legs.

Now that Alex had gained clarity regarding the direction he wanted to go in, I sent him off to write about his Ideal Job. From that very specific job, we crafted his message, his stories. From these stories, we used improv to make them come to life and really knock the socks off of recruiters and hiring managers.

Now that you have your ideal job, let's talk about how we can craft stories that you could share with a potential employer. These stories are your examples of successes and challenges. It is through these stories that you show that you can be a vital contributing member of their organization. That you are both in alignment with their culture and someone they can trust to get things done.

CHAPTER 5

Five Stories That Every Candidate Needs to Nail

I don't get controversial, I don't get political, and I don't tell you what to do with your life. I just go out there and tell some stories, and people can relate.
— GABRIEL IGLESIAS

Once you're clear about your direction, to the point of writing an ideal job posting, you're ready to create your personal stories—ones of passion, drive, grit, and success. This is my favorite part of the process because each of the stories is unique—beautiful peeks into the comprehensive history of your brilliance. In this chapter, I'll take you on a journey behind the curtain of recruiting to show you what recruiters really want to hear. Then, I'll share a methodology to help you design and refine five stories that every candidate needs to have. You can use this methodology for more than five (and I highly recommend you do). At the end of the chapter, I share other stories that you may want to create.

CONFESSIONS OF A RECRUITER

Having over 20 years of experience as a human resources recruiter, headhunter, and executive corporate recruiter, I'll share with you what might be going on behind the curtain. I'll share what I think might be going on at any point in the job search process—especially in the moments of deafening silence. One question that job seekers ask the most is, "What do recruiters want to hear?" That's easy. And it might not be what you think they want to hear. What recruiters want to hear is the *truth* of you. One myth to dispel is that candidates should try to answer questions in the way they think the recruiter wants to hear.

As a recruiter, I always start the interview with an easy question. I ask something to the effect of, "Tell me about your last role." It's an easy question because it's usually safe. They haven't delved deep into the harder subject of You. This easy lob over the net gets the candidate talking and more comfortable. And candidates who are comfortable are more honest. Recruiters want to know the real person. Their reputations are based on making great hires. In six months, the true person emerges from the hired candidate, and if that person is drastically different from the person the company thought they hired, the blame often falls on the recruiter. The more comfortable a person is early on in the interview process, the more of the true self is seen. Recruiters want to see that person early on to determine if that person would thrive in their company. Once the person is comfortable, the conversation slowly moves to the more difficult questions.

Whether your recruiter has the same process or not, you should be prepared to answer those more difficult questions. I am not talking about questions that dig deep into the technical aspects of the job. I am talking about the questions that delve deep into *you*. These questions tend to be vague and thus difficult to answer because you aren't sure what the recruiter wants to hear. Let us tell them about you. They want to know the *real* you.

QUESTIONS THAT ARE EASY AND QUESTIONS THAT ARE HARD

Melissa asked me why I never asked her about her previous work. "It is because I know you can answer that question with ease," I told her. Melissa laughed. "Yes, I would much prefer it if recruiters only asked me questions about my last job."

There are exceptions. There are situations where it is very important to review technical skill, especially if part of the interview process is assessment-based. For example, programmers will most often be faced with case studies of different programming challenges and then must, on the spot, attempt to program a solution. There are other jobs that require a similar type of preparation, like for a consulting position. In those instances, running through different case studies are important. However, in most other interviews where there isn't a history of these types of assessments, it is helpful to be prepared to answer those tough questions about you.

WHY QUESTIONS ABOUT YOU ARE HARD TO ANSWER

Questions about you are tough. Perhaps it is because many people don't really like talking about themselves. There's a comfort in talking about the other person. It could be from a deep sense of humility. Or, it could be from reading books like *How to Win Friends and Influence People* that suggest the best way to make a connection with someone is to be wildly curious about them. There may be times when you are surprised that the interviewer did all the talking; however, in many other cases, the tables are turned and you are sitting on the ask-me button. Or it could be a vague question like, "Tell me about yourself," that stumps you. And it could also be that you have so much experience, as mentioned before, that you don't know where to start. Whatever the reason, I have developed a guide to help you create answers to these vague questions about you.

EASY APPROACH TO HARD QUESTIONS

Many job seekers have found this easy approach to be helpful in answering tough questions. Although we cover five questions, I list other questions you may want to write stories for at the end of the chapter. You will eventually need to wing answers as recruiters are incredibly inventive in crafting different types of questions. At least with these five (and any more you create), you'll have these in your back pocket ready to provide. It will seem like you are pulling it out of thin air (like improv comedians), when in fact, the seemingly spontaneous response is a result of practice and process. In improv, when the audience is asked a suggestion, it may seem like off-the-wall suggestions; however, comedians know that audiences have their favorite things. We know that recruiters have favorite questions, too.

In almost every interview situation, these below questions are asked. Some exactly as stated or else very similar.

FAVORITE INTERVIEW QUESTION	WHAT THE RECRUITER WANTS TO KNOW
Tell me about yourself.	Anything to break the ice. Take advantage of the situation and answer in a deliberate way.
Tell me about your greatest achievement.	How much did this help the company? Scope. International? Size. 10 people or 1,000,000? How easy or hard?
Tell me about a time you've overcame a challenge.	Are you a doer? Do you have grit? Are you resourceful enough to get things done?

Describe a time you've worked within a team setting.	Will you cause trouble? Can you handle disruptors? Or do you ignore disruptors? Or are you a disruptor?
What is your greatest weakness?	Are you self-aware? Are you confident?

Let's take the "Tell me about yourself" question. Pull yourself out of job-seeking mode. Imagine that we are sitting at a café and I ask you, "How did you come to do what you're doing today? How did you select your profession? At what point in your life did you know you were supposed to do this? Have you always known? Or was it a slowly unfolding path?"

Step 1 – Write Out Your Answer

I recommend you use longhand to write your answers to these questions. There is something important that happens when you write out an answer (vs. typing on the computer)– you connect to a creative side of your brain. In fact, research says that when you write longhand, you use more parts of your brain than if you were to just type or speak. Find a nice clean sheet of ruled paper and grab your favorite writing utensil. (I love .7 2B lead mechanical pencils.) Sit and write as if I had casually asked you, "How did you get to where you are today?"

To give you an idea of how your story may flow, below is my rendition of Joy Behar's story, co-host of The View taken from two stories about Joy. (*New York Daily News*, May 3,

2017 and 5 True Stories of Real-Life Career Changers That'll Inspire You to Take That Leap, *Forbes*, December 23, 2015.)

> *My first job was cut-throat. I was a high school English teacher for 20 years. I used to teach high school in the toughest neighborhoods in New York City at that time. You know, the kind of kids who go to jail because they set fire to their neighbors. Kids would come to me to learn the difference between who and whom. I would try to make it relevant. I would say, "Whom do you wish to murder? Not who." Being an English school teacher prepared me well for the ruthless world of television. I was well into my forties when I returned to my childhood love of performing. I love being the co-host of The View. Little did I know that my stand-up gigs in front of my family would end up being a part of my beloved career. People should do what they loved to do when they were 10, the age before you start caring what others think.*

Step 2 – Time Your Story

The next step–after you've written out your story–is to tell your story aloud in a speed that is more akin to a story teller, and time yourself. Imagine yourself telling this story to someone who is in rapt attention. Add in pauses for effect. Vary the speed. Time yourself telling your story from start to finish. How long did it take you say the story in a normal voice and speed?

Joy's story took 50 seconds to read aloud.

Step 3 – Edit Your Story

If your story takes longer than 60 seconds to tell, edit it down. Type your story into the computer and edit. Cut out items that don't support the story. Add context, like who was there with you. What did it look like? Paint a picture. Describe it so that the listener is right there with you. Draw them in. A maximum of 60 seconds is the ideal length because you will likely lengthen it in an interview. It will be more conversational. We tend to add a bit to connect with the other person.

Another reason to keep it around 60 seconds is because some companies are now screening candidates with recorded videos instead of in-person interview. The system asks questions and you state answers of which you are recorded. The typical default tends to be 60 seconds to provide an answer.

Step 4 – Rehearse It

Congratulations in reaching this point! By this time, you have put a lot into creating your story. It is full of imagery and is compelling. In this step, you are cementing the story to memory. Practice saying this story at least 30 times in front of a mirror. Start out by reading it verbatim, using the full storytelling effects. Around the tenth time, you'll not need to read it verbatim.

Around the twentieth time, turn to a mirror and tell the story to yourself. Repeat the story at least ten more times and watch your face, your smile, and your mannerisms. Make tweaks so that you come across as you want to. It might feel awkward, as it is not often that we look at ourselves talking. Because job search interactions are almost always face to face, I recommend you look at yourself and ensure your mannerisms support how you want to come across.

My client Kathy sounded amazing over the telephone. She sounded brilliant and articulate—like a solid candidate. To help her prepare for her in-person interview, I scheduled a video call. During our video call, she sounded put together—but she was fidgeting. She was unable to sit still. She was touching her hair constantly. And she never looked me in the eyes. She looked nervous, despite the calmness of her voice.

Say your story in front of the mirror. See what recruiters will see when they speak with you.

BEFORE AND AFTER: TELL ME ABOUT YOURSELF

When I asked Daniel, "Tell me about yourself," he was in full interview mode. His answer was something like this:

Before: Daniel's Answer

I have been a rabbi for 30 years. I first started by leading the youth group in my father's congregation. Then I got my first rabbinical role at an organization where I led a congregation of 150 families. I was involved in the financial aspects of the congregation too, from fundraising to managing the books. I was also responsible to create curriculum, and then lead the congregation as its leader. Then, after that, I worked at a larger congregation of 500 families in Illinois. I left that role to lead a congregation here in this community. I was at this congregation for almost three years.

In general, this is the typical answer I get from job seekers. It's a chronological listing of their career. Sometimes the story starts from when they were born! It mirrors, for the most part, the chronology of the résumé. However, Daniel is not a typical person. And neither are you.

I told Daniel, "Ok, imagine we're not in an interview. What made you become a rabbi? Have you always known you wanted to be a rabbi?" Daniel lit up and told me an amazing story of how he became involved in the community through his rabbinical work and how that shaped his career choices.

After: Daniel's Answer

After college, I knew I wanted to serve my community so I became a police officer. Yes, I was one of "New York's finest." On the weekends, I volunteered at a local congregation leading the youth group. There I fell in love with congregation life and soon became a rabbi. Over the years, I've continued to serve my community through the congregation. In Chicago, after 9-11, I collaborated with four other churches and religious groups to create a day of prayer. We created a service full of healing and community between our Jewish congregation, a nearby mosque, Protestant, and Catholic Churches. This was the first of many inter-faith events I coordinated from New York to Chicago to San Francisco. Throughout my entire life, I've always known that I was meant to serve the community. And that's why I'm here today. I am very interested in the executive director role at your organization to build coalitions across the county.

Bullseye! Although the question isn't asking specifically for a story of your journey, this is exactly what a recruiter wants to hear. How you came to where you are today. If this is what the recruiter wants to hear, why don't they just ask that question? Good question! Some may. And for the others that do not, they'll usually go with "Tell me about yourself," which gives you an excellent opportunity to share your story with them. Like Daniel's story, one about how everything that has happened in his life has been intricately involved in bringing him to where he is today.

WHAT ABOUT THE OTHER FOUR QUESTIONS?

A key part of helping you write your stories is creating a different context by asking the question in different ways. Here are different contexts that may help you write your stories.

Tell Me About Yourself

Imagine you and I are at a sunny café. Or, imagine we are at a bar at happy hour. And I ask these questions…

How did you come to do what you're doing today? How did you select your profession? Did you always know? From childhood? If not, at what point in your life did you know you were supposed to do this? Was it an unfolding path?

How did you get from that to now? Is there a common thread or theme from then to now? What about what you do now makes you happy?

Tell Me About Your Greatest Achievement

Think about your current role or a recent role and tell me about a time you felt very proud of yourself. Whether you received external praise or not. A time you felt successful. A time you received an "atta-boy" or "atta-gal"? A time a client sent you a note or you walked out of a meeting feeling amazing. Pick the one that is a great success and write a story about it. Tell me as if you were describing the context, the setting, the people, and players. Tell me about the success and what was involved in getting to that achievement. Pull yourself out of interview mode and into storytelling mode. Set the stage for us.

Tell Me About a Time You Overcame a Challenge

Think of a time you faced an uphill battle or faced a task you thought you'd never complete. It could be something that was dropped in your lap with little training or support, or with limited budget and staff. But despite the setbacks, through your resourcefulness, you could pull it off. It could be something that occurred at the perfect time, or an opportunity that would have passed by without you taking initiative.

Describe a Time You've Worked Within a Team Setting

This is an opportunity to describe your ability to work with all sorts of people–characters of all levels, titles, departments, and personalities. You can create a story of someone who was difficult to work with. Yet despite it all, you got the work done. It could be a team that worked extremely well to complete a task. Or a team that you pulled together over time–hiring members that resulted in a dynamic group. Thinking of shying away from talking about difficult people? As a recruiter, I made it a point to ask specifically about working with someone who was difficult. When the answer is, "I never did." I begin to wonder if that could possibly be true.

One job seeker, Melissa, stuck to her guns. "No, I've never worked with anyone difficult." I asked in a different way if she worked with someone who didn't pull their weight or didn't pitch in at the same level as others. When I continued to ask questions, perhaps appearing as if I wasn't going to move from this point, she recalled someone in a work team who didn't pull his weight. I wondered if she didn't say anything earlier because she thought it wouldn't look good. Of course, I then began to wonder what else she didn't mention.

You may not have had a serious problem with someone, but we've all worked with someone who made it just a little bit more challenging. The recruiter wants to hear how you handled the situation. Did you address it directly? Or work around the person? Both completely reasonable depending on the culture and situation.

Tell Me What Is Your Greatest Weakness

In one shape or another, you will be asked this question: "What is your greatest weakness?" It might be in the form of the question, "Tell me your strengths and weaknesses." I've even heard it asked, "In six months we'll know you well. What should we know about you now?" The reason recruiters ask this is twofold. One, recruiters do not like surprises. We are rated on our ability to introduce talent that will, in the long-term, be great for the organization and productive for the team. Two, we want to know if you are self-aware.

Recruiters in Human Resources discuss this issue at great lengths, and many assessments help companies identify whether a candidate is self-aware. We believe that 99% of all performance issues stem from someone who is not self-aware. They are not honest with themselves and/or not honest with others. Miscommunication occurs as a result, and then human resources is called to try to salvage the situation. We want to know the degree of your self-awareness so that we can avoid a lot of heartache in the long run. Because of this, I recommend you share your true weakness.

When I asked Daniel what his greatest weakness is, this was his answer:

> *From what I've seen and what I've been told, my greatest weakness is that I live an unbalanced work–life situation. I tend to work too much and it infringes on my personal life and that is not good.*

Some form of workaholism is the #2 top answer recruiters hear when we ask this question. The #1 answer? "I'm a perfectionist." The worst answer? "I can't think of any." These answers do not sit well with a recruiter because they are, for the most part, not true. And we can sense that something is amiss. Our faces leak our feelings. In an interview, the organization is looking for people they can bring into their organization, their tribe, and the fundamental need is trust. Because of this, and the fact that they will see your greatest weakness within the first few months of you starting anyway, it's best to be transparent from the start.

What is interesting about your greatest weakness is that is has helped you. Whether it has caused you to compensate by developing a counter-balancing skill or helped you improve your self-awareness, your greatest weakness isn't as negative as you may think. I position it this way with job seekers: Imagine that we are not in an interview. We are friends sitting at a bar and I ask, "So, what do you really think is your greatest weakness?"

Kathy's self-proclaimed greatest weakness was her anxiety. She got very anxious about things and she knew that this hindered her in many ways. She second guessed herself. She wondered how other people saw her. She could get very caught up in the "what ifs" of a situation, and she knew that it came through in the interview process. And if asked about her greatest weakness, the last thing she wanted to do was disclose this; however, I encouraged her to do so. "How in the world do I disclose this without looking undesirable?"

she asks. Together we created this honest, real answer to the question, "Tell me your greatest weakness."

> *I can get anxious about things—new situations, scenarios, things that are high stakes, or seemingly high stakes. Even now during this interview I am quite anxious! This comes out in many ways, from thinking of all the negative things that could go wrong to going overboard in preparing for tests at school to rehearsing ad nauseum for presentations. I'm quite aware of this about myself and used to think it was debilitating; however, what I've realized is that, in a strange way, it has helped me learn how to channel anxiety in positive ways. I go to great lengths to ensure that I am prepared. It is something I've come to terms with about myself, and I continue to find positive ways to channel that nervous energy. And, in many ways, it helps in the field of clinical research and medical writing—fields that demand accuracy.*

In her answer, she is transparent about her self-proclaimed and believed weakness. She talks about how she works to combat this weakness so that it's a non-issue and talks about how, in some instances, the weakness is helpful.

Now it is up to the recruiter to consider: Is this a weakness this team can live with? I would say that it depends. What if the manager is high-strung, and putting the two together would be a very volatile working situation? Or perhaps the manager is also very self-aware and together they'd find a lot of common ground. Or if the manager needs help with details, she might love this weakness of Kathy's. Essentially, you don't know if your weakness will work or not for the team. I would trust that if they were to move forward with the interview process, they believe that your weakness is something they can live with (and maybe even need). And with your authenticity, you are rewarded with the sense of being true to yourself and to them. Conversely, it may not be the environment *you* want.

What if there is another anxiety-ridden leader on the team that you would clash with a lot? It might not be the best situation for you to thrive in. You know what you want. You are more transparent with what you want, what you can do, what you will do, and quite frankly, what you are not willing to do. This question of fit is a powerful one, as it helps job seekers gain clarity on the type of environment they want. Daniel, for instance, called me disappointed that he didn't get a job offer. He said that the recruiter, whom he connected well with from the start, said that the team was hoping for someone with a tremendous level of high energy. I asked Daniel if he could be that high energy every day on the job. "Well, if you put it that way, maybe it wasn't a great fit," he said.

When you lean into your greatest weakness, beautiful stories of vulnerability and authentic self-reflection are told. Sometimes it's like a pressure cooker valve has been released. Just talking about your greatest weakness can bring a wonderful sense of contentment and acceptance (and love). I highly recommend you give the true answer because your face will give you away if you offer a false answer. We can detect minor minuscule hints that someone may not be telling the truth. Tiny movements of the face and eyes, too much or too little eye contact, a little shift here and there and we get a gut feeling that perhaps the person is not quite telling the truth. It is so powerful to be real. Embrace who you are because when I look at you, I see a rock star. An incredible person with amazing talent doing such great things for this world.

OTHER QUESTIONS TO ANSWER

If you would like to take the methodology of creating stories beyond the five, here are a few other questions (and rephrasing of the questions) to help you create more stories. The more stories you have simmering at the surface, the more material you'll have to share during interactions with recruiters.

Achievements

Tell me about a time a customer/client thanked you for a job well done.

Tell me about a time when you mentored someone who rose to great heights.

Tell me about a time you saved the day.

Tell me about a time you felt on top of the world at work.

Tell me about a time you worked on something that took a long time to pull together.

Overcoming an Obstacle

Tell me about a time you did something against the odds.

Tell me about a time when you worked on a project that was doomed to fail, but you were instrumental in making it successful.

Tell me about a time when you didn't think you'd be able to get something done, but you were able to in the end.

Tell me about a time you were given a task and the person assigning it said, "I doubt you'll be able to do this."

Getting Along

Tell me about a time you worked within a team and your team achieved great things.

Tell me about a time you worked with someone who was difficult to work with and how you made it work.

Tell me about a time you worked on a team that was low-functioning and you made it work.

Tell me about a time you had to work with someone that was disruptive and how you overcame the situation.

Tell me about a time you worked on a team and there was someone who didn't pull his or her weight, and how you helped the team achieve.

Tell me about a team that worked incredibly well together.

WHAT QUESTIONS ARE YOU CONCERNED ABOUT?

Use this methodology to prepare for other questions, particularly the ones you are the most concerned about getting asked. When I ask job seekers, "What are you afraid they will ask you?" I hear questions that aren't exactly easy to answer. It could be about being fired from a job, a long gap between jobs, or why you left a company after only 3 months. Below are a few examples of questions that you might be dreading in the job search process and ways in which you could tackle them to create an authentic story to respond that still puts you in the best light.

Situation: I Was Pushed Out and Don't Know Why

Kathy left her medical writing job after eight months. In the industry, this is seen as a euphemism for saying that she was fired, and an obvious red flag. It's hard to make it as a medical writer, and they know that the ones who struggle do not last their first year. Kathy thought that she bore the responsibility of her termination; however, as we talked about the circumstances of her departure, it was clearly a company financial decision. It took a bit of reframing because Kathy, being a very accountable person, assumed that it must be her fault somehow.

She told me, "It was a really bad time for me. I had some tough personal situations occur and my mind wasn't fully focused on my job and plus, I was not sure I really liked medical writing and it probably showed. I always wondered if it was performance related."

I asked, "What reason did they give for why you were being let go?"

"Lack of work. I was told that we lost two big pieces of business and that they didn't have enough work for me," said Kathy.

"Did they let anyone else go?"

"Yes, two of us were let go."

"Did they treat you well when you left?"

"Yes. I could tell my boss was sad that he had to tell me that my job was ending. He was on the verge of tears. I still keep in touch with people there."

"Kathy, you were not fired. You were laid off. If they fired you, they wouldn't be sad to see you leave."

Together we wrote the below answer for when a recruiter asks, "Why did you stay only eight months at your last employer?"

My manager and other members of the company told me that the amount of work for the medical writing team was shrinking. I found out that the company had lost two major clients the quarter before. Another member of our team and I, the two newest team members, were let go. It was sudden and sad and I could tell that my manager was very sad to see me go. I'm glad I had the chance to learn from the senior medical writers. And it has become a blessing in disguise, as this has reignited my love of clinical research. I don't think I would've come to this conclusion on my own until several years down the line, as I would've been head-down in the world of medical writing. Although it felt tough at the time, I now look back and see that it was a good thing for me.

If you are worried that you'll be asked a certain question, I recommend you bounce off the situation with someone who knows the behind-the-scenes activities of human resources or something similar. There are many reasons why things happen to end employment, and by asking a few questions, you can learn the truth. And if you were truly fired, I recommend you design an answer that is both honest and puts you in the best light.

Situation: I Was Fired

Speaking with Jeremy, I understood that he was clearly fired. It was the classic situation: Friday at 5 pm with the urgent last-minute meeting in the conference room. When he walked in, there was his boss and the VP of HR with a small packet of documents in front of them. Telling the story was still very bitter for Jeremy, and I could hear it in his voice.

"Over 10 years ago, I was the only provider in the practice. I worked with the administration to fix things that were time-wasters to the operations. And over time I hired more providers. Together, we built the practice to a healthy and thriving center that became the model for other practices across the US. One of the guys I brought on board was particularly ambitious. We argued about something and I stepped over the line and said things to him that I regret. I apologized afterwards, but the damage was already done. He formed a particularly close relationship with the CEO and, over time, my power was slowly etched away. Once we hit a certain revenue number, the CEO apparently wasn't interested in additional growth–and so when I proposed a path for growth, he made it clear that his objective now was to maintain status quo, ride this wave if possible. I get that. However, I am a change agent. And I guess I continued to push instead of finding another practice that needed a rain maker. And the other provider that I had an argument with was promoted above me, now reporting directly to the CEO. And I knew my days were numbered. Then came the ill-fated day that they called me into the conference room to fire me."

How do you turn that situation into an honest answer that can put Jeremy in the best light? One thing you should know about Jeremy is that he is a super star. He is a rain maker. He knows how to grow practices from struggling to exponential growth in revenues and reputation. His company no longer needed him. His magic was needed somewhere else. This is the honest transparent answer that we created. Today, Jeremy is head of another practice that is struggling, and he is their rain maker that will take them to new heights. Together we designed an authentic honest answer.

When I started with the practice, it was struggling to survive. We were experiencing declining margins and the practice had to let go all of the providers except me. I saw the situation as a significant opportunity. Together with the CEO, we turned the practice into a multimillion dollar revenue generating practice that is doing exciting innovative things in care and care delivery. At a certain point, it was clear that we had not only saved the practice but put it on a very strong path. After years of continued growth, the CEO and board decided that it wouldn't be in the best interest of the practice to continue to grow, and I became restless because of that. The bug to grow practices was born within me. They knew that I wouldn't be satisfied with status quo and they gave me time to look for another practice, somewhere I could do the same thing. At first it was tough to swallow because of what I invested in the company. I've poured over 12 years into this practice. But what I realized is that they were right. I would've continued to be frustrated pushing growth where it wasn't needed any longer. It is time for me to do the same for another practice.

Now you will notice that Jeremy didn't say that he was fired. He did say that his services weren't needed any longer. If pushed, Jeremy would've said that he received a generous severance package and a commitment from leadership to support him in his next move. Which is absolutely the case. I wouldn't advise anyone to say that they were outright fired. It is a loaded word that conjures the worst, "You're Fired!" images. And rarely are terminations actually at that abrupt end of the spectrum. However, if you *were* at that end of the spectrum, for example, terminated due to theft, inappropriate use of company equipment, etc. and have come to terms with the situation, I recommend you discuss this with your career coach to come up with an honest authentic answer that communicates where you are today versus then.

Many job seekers have at least one of these difficult questions to answer. The process of writing it out, timing it, editing it, rehearsing in front of a mirror at least 30 times, is the same process for each of the situations and questions. Once you have these stories very close to your skin, you are ready to take the next step and put them to practice and bring these stories to life. In the next chapter, we're going to play a few games. Improv games. Here is where it starts to get fun and a little bit crazy! Let's go!

CHAPTER 6

Make Your Stories Come to Life

Laughter heals all wounds, and that's one thing that everybody shares. No matter what you're going through, it makes you forget about your problems. I think the world should keep laughing.
– KEVIN HART

I love doing improv with job seekers. It is so much fun, and although we aren't intending to be funny, we always end up laughing–at ourselves, at what was just said, at the situation. It is certainly a stretching experience to do improv. In the context of a coaching session, it feels very safe. It is just the two of us. If, at the end of this book, you want to venture out a little more, I recommend that you join an improv class to experience it in a group setting. Not all improv makes sense for the job search process. I've culled the list of games to ones that are very relevant to our world–increasing charisma by playing big, being intentional with your eye contact, and staying connected through mime. Jump on a video call with your coach. Or ask a friend to play some of these improv games with you. Through this process we learn a little more about ourselves as it forces to be right here, right now, present. Let's play!

IMPROV GAMES THAT HELP WITH BODY CONTROL

Game: Play Big and Play Small

Imagine there are two chairs up on stage. You are sitting in one of the chairs and an improv partner is sitting next to you. The two of you are facing an audience. The lights are glaring in your eyes and you can see shadows of people sitting in the audience watching the two of you. Your job is to play big without saying a word or making a sound. Sitting on the chair with the use of communicating big with your body, you are to claim that space. Your improv partner next to you is playing small. Using his body, without saying a word, he is playing small. The goal is for you to play big and slowly transform to small over a period of 30 seconds. The teacher in the audience will tell you when it is 15 seconds and when it is time at 30 seconds. Your improv partner's goal is to do exactly the opposite. He is to play small and transform to big over 30 seconds.

Terri and I use video meetings for this game. She starts with being big and I start with being small. In 30 seconds, we switch back and forth from being big to being small.

You can do this at home. Place a chair in front of a mirror and play big. Put on a timer that signals at 30 seconds. And over that period, without saying a word, transform to play small. Pay attention to how you feel when you are playing big and when you are playing small. Try it!

When I asked Terri to explain what she did when she played big, this is what she said:

- I am sitting up
- My shoulders are back
- My legs are spread and out in front of me
- My arms are draped over the arms of my improv partner's chair
- I am looking directly ahead
- I am looking around directly into my partner's eyes

When I asked Terri to explain how she felt when she was playing big, this is what she said:

- Confident
- Big
- Aggressive
- In control
- In charge
- The boss

I asked Terri, what did you feel when you were playing small?

- Timid
- Scared
- Submissive
- Anxious
- Cautious

Give it a try. For an entire week, play big. And take note at how you feel.

Game: Control Your Eye Contact

Because we do not go through life looking in a mirror, we often aren't aware of how we communicate with our eyes. We may not know that our eyes might be moving constantly or that we might come across as staring. This improv game is one that helps us become aware of our eyes and gain control over what we want to communicate with them.

Imagine you are in a room with your hypothetical improv team. Half of the team, Team A, has a goal to give what they would consider to be intense or too-long eye contact. The other half, Team B, has a goal to avoid eye contact or give too-short eye contact. When the game starts, everyone is to walk around the room acting out their goal. You'll hear nervous laughter and all-out bursts of laughter as two Team A members have a staring contest. Then about 2 minutes into the game, the instructor tells everyone to switch. Team A's job is to avoid all eye contact and Team B's goal is to give intense eye contact. At around two minutes more, the teacher calls time.

In a coaching session, the coach's goal is to give intense eye contact and the client's goal is to give not enough, or fleeting eye contact. Then we switch after 30 seconds.

At home, you could ask a friend to play the role of the coach. Sitting across a table, designate someone to give intense and the other fleeting eye contact. Use a timer and switch after 30 seconds.

Then we debrief and ask to share what happened and what made them laugh, how they felt, which was the most comfortable for them. Typically, the answers are something like the below:

- If I am avoiding eye contact, it is uncomfortable when someone gives me intense eye contact. It feels like an invasion of my space. It feels too intense.
- But when I am the one giving intense eye contact, it is frustrating when someone is avoiding my eye contact.
- It is a bit more comfortable if I meet with someone who is also giving intense eye contact, but if it goes too long, it feels uncomfortable.
- When I am avoiding eye contact and come across someone who is also avoiding, it feels good not to be stared at; however, I do not even see who that person was.

In a coaching session, I will share if I feel that the individual gives a comfortable amount of eye contact. It is a challenge over video conference, and the fact that we aren't looking in a camera at eye level and instead at the person on the screen. However, it is excellent practice since many job interviews are conducted over video conference.

This game helps people understand how it feels when appropriate intensity of eye contact is given. It gives people the opportunity to play around with too much and too little to have greater control over when it is just enough.

Game: Staying Connected Through Mime

A mime is an actor who is generally in black and white clothing, with white clown paint on their face. They act out different things without using their voice. Imagine you are standing in a large circle with other people and you are all mimes. One person starts by holding an imaginary object and doing something obvious with the object. It could be bouncing a basketball or kicking a soccer ball. He then passes or hands the object to his neighbor who then continues doing what his neighbor did with the object. Then he changes it up. Perhaps the basketball shrinks and become a tennis ball. That person then passes or hands the object to the next person. And it goes down the line.

As you can image, sometimes you have no idea what your partner just did. The actions aren't always obvious and you need to make sense of the action. And you'll also realize that it is fruitless to think of something to do ahead of time because you won't know what the object is until it is handed to you.

This game forces us to use our bodies in intentional ways to describe the object and do something with it. It also helps you learn how to not anticipate what you will do with the object because you have no idea in what form the object will come to you. Learning not to anticipate and just be in the moment is one of the most useful things improv can help with in the job search process. It drives out the habit of spinning in your own head. You must just be in the moment.

In a coaching session, I start with an object, do something obvious, and then hand it to the job seeker. She takes it, continues with what I was doing and then does something different and hands it back to me.

At home, you can ask a friend to do the same where you start with an object, do something obvious, and then hand it to your friend. She takes it, continues with what you were doing and then does something different and hands it back to you.

Here are a few ideas of things that you could do with your improv group, whether in a large group or in a pair:

- Eat a lollipop
- Eat a popsicle
- Eat an ice cream cone
- Throw a volleyball
- Throw a baseball
- Use a home phone
- Use a mobile phone

IMPROV GAMES THAT HELP WITH VOICE CONTROL

The greatest comedian I've ever seen is Jack Benny. He
wasn't afraid of the silences.
− BOB NEWHART

Now that you have learned improv games that help you have greater awareness and control of your body, let's focus on your voice. When you combine body and voice control, you are on your way to making a very powerful in-person impression. Voice control is critical to get invited to a face-to-face interview. Many companies will first want to speak with you over the telephone before they make the investment in coordinating an in-person interview. And I've found that many job seekers aren't sure how they come across over the telephone. They think they are showing up in one way, but my impression of them is slightly, or sometimes very, different.

Many of my clients are across the nation so it is impractical to meet them in person. The first time I see them is always a wonderful surprise, as I'm seeing someone that I've grown to love over a period. It is always a wonderful surprise to finally see someone's animated face and not just an image, like a photo from their LinkedIn profile. And I am always surprised that the person is nothing like I had expected. Which goes to show that when we only speak with a recruiter, they also form an impression of what you look like that is often very different from what you actually look like. The idea is to control that impression as much as you can. Below are a few improv games you can play to gain greater voice control.

Because improv feeds off at least one other person, most improv games are best done within a pair or a group. Improv is an interactive sport. Here are a few improv games that you can play solo if you have a device that can record what you are saying (e.g., smartphone).

Game: Talking Fast and Slow

In high school, I was running for a state position for a national business organization. While I was practicing my speech, my dad kept saying, "Slow down!" It was a struggle to really slow it down. I thought it was so people could follow along with what I was saying; however, what I discovered is that we make assumptions about someone's competence by the speed of their speech. Research says that people who speak slowly appear to be more competent and intelligent.

Use your mobile device or another recording device for this game. Grab some nearby text and record yourself reading it. At first, read it fast, much faster than your normal speech rate, and record yourself. Then read the same page again at a rate slower than your normal speech rate. Play back both recordings and see the difference in how you come across speaking quickly and slowly.

In improv, comedians use voice control to support a certain character they are playing. They will speed up when it serves them. In the same way, you want to be mindful of the rate of your speech so that you support how you wish to come across. For the most part, you will be speaking slowly and clearly to support the fact that you are competent and in control.

Related to speed is the power of the pause. Pauses can be used wisely to make a point. Consider this sentence and placement of the pause: "That project was the turning point for our division. [pause] We saw revenues climb at a steady pace from that point. And I cannot emphasize how vital our cohesion was to our success. Without it [pause] we would have failed."

Try it on for size. For an entire day, be very deliberate in speaking slower than your normal rate and see how it feels. And throw in a few pauses [pause] to make a point.

Game: High and Low

Besides the speed of your speaking, the pitch is also important. Individuals who have a high vocal pitch are seen in a different way than individuals with a lower pitch. People who speak at a higher pitch come across as less confident. Conversely, people with a lower pitch come across as more confident, dominant.

Let's play another improv game with your recording device. Read another page from a book in a pitch that is slightly higher than your normal pitch and record yourself. Do the same and read with a slightly lower pitch than normal. Listen to both recordings and take note of how you come across.

Give it a go. Spend an entire day speaking in a lower pitch than your normal. How did that feel?

Another thing to think about is if you end your sentences on an up note–when your voice goes higher as if you are asking a question. I find that often people aren't aware when they tend to end their sentences on an up note. As with the speed and the pitch, the tendency may leave an impression that you don't want. Research shows that individuals who end their sentences on an up note come across as less confident and more subservient, always seeking approval. Of course, this is not necessarily the case if this is your tendency. Many of my clients who have this tendency are strong, assertive, and confident. They just aren't aware how they come across.

Controlling your voice in and of itself is helpful in the job search process as many of the screening interviews are done over the telephone–no visual used. Combined with body control, you now offer a very powerful package. Let us now mix it in with the stories that were created in the previous chapter and put it all together.

INTEGRATE BODY AND VOICE CONTROL WITH YOUR CHARACTER: YOU

During Steve Martin's Masterclass, he encourages comedians to leverage what makes us unique, saying, "There is room for you." In his world, to use our uniqueness contributes to being hilarious. And that holds true for our work as well. To use our uniqueness to be amazing.

Sitting in a room with Jenny, an impressive Communications Specialist, I was heartbroken, as it was obvious to her (and everyone else) that the Vice-President was about to push her out. To me, she was amazing. And it was clear that this organization was not a great fit for her–her unique and creative, out-of-the-box ideas landed too often on glazed faces. Jenny soon left the company and took a job in a firm with the perfect culture for her. She is now the Director of Communications for a global financial services firm reporting to the CEO and creating the most innovative stuff in the field of corporate communications.

There is room for you. Let us mix in You by using improv. First by putting on the skin of someone who is completely out of character for you.

Game: Get Into Character

Let's have some fun and pull these things together with a few improv games. Let us try on a few skins of other people that may be very different from us. Take one of the characters below and imagine yourself putting on their skin. Say the below paragraph in that character using body and voice control to become the character. Try not to break and burst out in laughter. Stay in character. Practice what we've learned in body and voice control to become the person.

Say this paragraph in character. Watch YouTube clips of others in this persona to practice a few times and try it.

It is a beautiful day. The sun is shining and the birds are singing. I'm excited to be alive!

- 16-year-old Valley Girl from California–It's like so beautiful. Like totally kicking. Like the sun is amaaaazing. I'm so, like, you know, OMG, alive.
- Gun slinging, swaggering cowboy in the wild, wild west– (burst through the saloon doors, take a swig from your cigarette and flick it to the floor) Well, if it

ain't a pretty day. Sun was shining in my eyes as I shot a bird singing. A good day to be alive.

- A cranky, crusty, pessimistic old man–Pffft. Don't give me all this crap about it being a beautiful day. Stupid sun shining in my eyes. Damned birds singing. Shut up. Not a good day to be alive.

- A 30-foot giant–Fi fi fo fum. It's a beauuutiful day for some delicious bird. Cook it in the sun. Feed my big hungry belly to say alive.

- Martin Luther King, Jr.–I have a dream. One day, one beautiful day. The sun will shine and the birds will sing. We. Will. All. Be. Alive.

- A pirate–Avast you scurvy scum. Shiver me timbers, the sun's out. It's a blimey sunny day. Me burd danced the hampen jig. Son of a biscuit eater.

WHAT IS YOUR CHARACTER? CREATE AN ARCHETYPE

Now that we are donning the skins of other characters, let us talk about our own archetype for the interview: You. What is the skin that we will put on as we enter the interview space? The skin of You?

A few years back, I attended a coach training class. On the second day we did a remarkable thing. Carey Baker, instructor extraordinaire, pulled me on stage and asked everyone to throw out a few words or phrases of things people wanted to see more of from me. What was remarkable was that up until this point, we haven't spent a tremendous amount of time together. How could they possibly know me that well? Yet my fellow classmates were throwing out words and phrases at such a fast speed that someone had to write them down for me. This is the list:

- Adventure
- Break the rules
- Be brave
- Step out
- Be irresponsible

Then Carey asked the group to think of a personality or an archetype that they would like to see me put on. Many archetypes were thrown out, but the one that really stuck with them (I had no say in the selection, by the way) was Motorcycle Mama.

Yes! That is perfect! Motorcycle Mama. We want more of Motorcycle Mama from you, Cara. Jump on your hog and screech out of here, leaving a trail of dust in our faces.

I've since renamed this archetype to be Motorcycle Mama, and over the years have put on this skin when I've needed to be big and a bit of a rebel. And over time, this persona has become more a part of me. So, what is your archetype?

Here are a few archetypes of some of my clients.

- Oprah Winfrey
- Adonis the god of war
- Purring sexy black panther
- Pele, the fire goddess of the Hawaiian Islands
- James Bond
- Dr. Love

If you need help finding your archetype, send me a note, and let's get on the phone. I love helping people find their archetype, and you'll be amazed at how you can do this after a very short conversation.

IT'S SHOW TIME – LET'S PUT IT ALL TOGETHER

Put on your skin of You, your archetype. Answer the question, "Tell me about yourself." Use your body control and your voice control. Get into the character, stand in front of a mirror, and now rehearse. How is it different in character? Bigger? Bolder? Many job seekers say that they are much more aware of how they come across. And even more important, they can control how they come across. Their stories are more vivid with pauses for effect. Using silence. To make a point.

Ask your coach or a friend to conduct a mock interview. Record the session. Go back and view it. Refine your pitch, your skit, your stories. Ensure that you are coming across as you intend. Powerfully you. You have the tools to show up in a very powerful way. A way that is authentic and true to you. Showing them that you are secure in who you are, what you stand for, and what you can accomplish for them. And with a new awareness of You, your archetype, the skin of which you don as you prepare for and enter conversations with a recruiter. What we've talked about up until this point is how you show up. But as we know, it takes two to tango. There is someone else in the conversation: the recruiter, or the hiring manager, or other members of the team that you will interact with along the way. The next chapter provides tips and tools to bring that other person or people into the conversation in a way that leaves them feeling very connected to you. You'll leave them thinking about you and being attracted to you, a person who is confident and full of grace.

CHAPTER 7

Sometimes What You Don't Say Speaks the Loudest

I can't just say the words, do a lot of one-liners.
I love each person I play. I have to be that person.
I have to do him true.
– RICHARD PRYOR

Nick Saban is one of the best college football coaches of all time. Every article I've read about him always starts with recruiting–he is considered one of the best college football recruiters–starting from members on his coaching staff to every player on his team. He goes to great lengths to learn about players beyond just size and speed. He wants to know their personality, their weaknesses, and if the player will make their team better.

What can we learn from Nick Saban? Interviewers are looking for more than people who meet the qualifications of the job. Organizations want someone who will make the team better, stronger, more profitable, more successful. That takes looking at things that are not on a résumé. Hearing what is not being said. Getting to the heart of someone so that the person who shows up on the first day is the same person they thought they were hiring.

As a recruiter, when I sit with a hiring manager, I push aside the job description and ask, "What do you want that is not written on the job description?" I take note of a long list of things that have more to do with traits or the personality of someone than knowledge, skills, or experience. Here are some of those characteristics that are often desired by hiring managers, but not listed on a job posting:

- Someone who will stick around and not leave for a higher-paying job in a year–passionate about what we are passionate about
- A person with grit who will not be stymied by rejection or failure–figures out ways to get things done
- A team player, someone who knows how to work with people, when to speak up, when to stay silent–no Machiavellian power plays

- Someone with a positive disposition who won't poison the rest of the team with negativity—refrains from complaining or talking negatively about others
- A person who is grounded, self-aware, confident in their own abilities and in tune to limitations—won't cover up mistakes or tell me what they think I want to hear

You've designed at least five amazing stories and learned improv techniques to have greater control over your body and voice so that, when you wear the skin of your archetype, a fuller You shines through as you tell your stories. You've done an amazing job of creating the words and learning how things are articulated. Let us continue along this path and focus on how things are said.

Humans have an uncanny ability to see through other people. Have you ever been in a situation when you could tell the person you were talking to was hiding something? It might've been a slight hesitation in one of their responses. Or the way they looked up through the corner of their eyes. The cue could be so incredibly small, yet we tend to notice it.

I call these "tells" our leaky face. Our face leaks. Even the most trained improv comedian or actor has a leaky face.

Your ability to come across as authentic is critical. If you're reading this book, you're not looking for quick fixes or the easy answer. You are willing to work hard and do what it takes to get a job with meaning. Because of that, I know certain things about you—you are honest, you are hardworking, you have grit, you play fair, you are a great person to have on a team. This chapter is about making those characteristics come through loud and clear during the interview process. And it starts with making a strong connection with the interviewer, listening (really listening) to them, being focused on others (which is so hard in an interview), and being true to you.

HOW TO CONNECT WITH YOUR INTERVIEWERS

Earlier I mentioned Dale Carnegie and his international best-selling book, *How to Win Friends and Influence People*. It is considered one of the best self-help books ever published. At the time of Dale Carnegie's death, he had sold over five million copies and translated into 31 languages. What I love about this book is that if you wish to win people to your side, Carnegie suggests, the secret is to become *genuinely* interested in them. This is antithetical to the interview. In the interview, you are supposed to be the center of inquiry and attention, not them. Yet to connect and win the interviewer to your side, you are to switch your focus from your achievements to them. Every perspective and answer is filtered through how it would help them.

Darren was a rare breed in the facilities space. With a background in furniture design, fine arts, and theater, he saw all facilities as blank canvases on which to create beautiful functional spaces. His 15-plus years in facilities with exceptional longevity at each company and his Master of Science in Construction and Facilities Management degree made him a unique and highly sought-after talent in the facilities world. Yet he struggled in the interviews.

Recovering from a tough political fight between his boss and a peer, Darren was squeezed out of the organization at his last job. Although his immediate boss wrote an incredible letter of reference and remained open to explaining to any new hiring leader why Darren was let go, Darren carried the shame of–for the first time in his career–being laid-off. As he interviewed with hiring managers, he overcompensated. He pushed his achievements because he felt like he had to counterbalance the reason for leaving. As a result, he came across as cocky and arrogant. Darren is anything but. He is humble and cares deeply for others.

How do you come across as you intend to? Here are a few tips to help you win interviewers over to your side.

Listen. Really Listen.

Often in a conversation, while someone else is speaking, we are busy. Instead of being present and listening, we are busy formulating our reply. You'd think this would be a good thing in an interview. The problem is, the person you are talking to can tell you really aren't listening. There are a few clues that trigger me as a recruiter in an interview when someone may be a poor listener.

- They answer something that I talked about two sentences ago and not the current topic
- They interrupt me when I am speaking
- They talk over me while I am speaking

When this occurs, I write this in my interviewer notes, "Listening???" It is a major red flag. And if I am speaking with a Darren, the reason might not be that he isn't a good listener, it could be some other factor. How do you stay present and listen?

This is where improv is very valuable. In improv, you don't know what is going to happen next. Everything happens in the moment. There is little sense to formulate a response in your head. In improv, you stay very present until it is time to act.

Vanessa has been with her company for over 15 years, and after three years in a leadership role, she was demoted. One of the reasons was feedback from employees that she was a poor listener. Over video conference, we played these improv lessons. And within two short weeks, her team noticed a difference, enough to say something to executive leadership. Let us play some of those improv games for you to work on your listening skills.

Improv Lesson: Yes, And...

This game can be played in a pair or in a group circle. One person starts the game by saying a sentence. The next person must start his sentence with, "yes, and" and adds a sentence to continue the previous thought. Because it is impossible to know exactly how the sentence will end, the next person must listen to the entire sentence before he responds.

This game teaches people to wait until the other person has completed their sentence before speaking. It also teaches the power of the word "and." As a leader, you know the power of your words. Your words have great impact. Not just little ripples in a pond, your words have the weight of waves crashing against the shore. There isn't a word that stops creativity more quickly than the word BUT. I'm sure you've heard the saying: Anything that is said before the "but" is negated once that word is uttered. The same goes for improv, where creativity and being funny on the fly is essential. Comedians are trained early on to keep a conversation going. Similarly, in the interview, keeping a conversation going is a skill that can leave a recruiter feeling that it was a great meeting rather than one that was awkward or one-sided.

Let us take a work scenario and see this in effect. The setting is a performance review. The leader tells her employee, "You've had a great year, but I'd like you to focus on strengthening your team dynamics." Compare that to the exact same sentence with one word changed. "You've had a great year; and I'd like you to focus on strengthening your team dynamics." One word gives a positive and encouraging feeling to the feedback.

The interview is the same. Practice the "Yes, and" game with someone so that you create a new habit of listening and conveying a positive feeling by using the word "and." The lesson, "yes, and" also has another side effect: by continuing with their previous thought, it validates the other person's ideas. This validation is the next lesson of making the other person feel brilliant.

MAKE THE OTHER PERSON BRILLIANT

Often in interviews, we want to come across as brilliant. We want to show how smart we are. We want them to know we have a MBA or MD and graduated at the top of the class. However, should we?

I've often said that the job search process is like dating. Imagine that you are on a date and the other person is talking about how smart he is, how brilliant he is, how much education he has, and how knowledgeable he is. It is such a big turn-off. In the same way, when we share successes, we want the company to be the winner, the team to be successful, and colleagues to be brilliant. Compare these two answers to the question, "Why do you want to work for us?"

Answer A: I believe my ten years as an executive recruiter where I've hired hundreds of people is a testament to my talents. That plus my Master's degree from Cornell makes me the perfect person for the job.

Answer B: I've been watching your company for several years. I believe my years as an executive recruiter where our team has hired hundreds of people can help your company fill critical roles. I'll bring my knowledge to your recruiting team so that together we add talent and capabilities to the company.

The second answer is about *them*. How you've been following them and want to make them successful. That you've done that in the past and can do that for them. The focus is on them.

Here is a game that puts the emphasis on the other person winning.

Game: Change Three Things

This hilarious improv game is done in a pair. It is easier in person; however, you could play this game on a video chat. Face your partner and memorize everything you can about the person's appearance. You have 20 seconds to memorize everything. Then turn away from each other and change three things about your appearance. It could be moving your hair part in another direction. Your goal is to make your partner brilliant so you want to change things that should be incredibly obvious. Then on a count of three turn to face one another and point out the three changes. Change partners, if in a group. This changes the paradigm that in this game you want the other person to win.

As an executive recruiter, I was very much tuned in to finding great listeners. The more I felt listened to, the more connected I became to the candidate. Hand in hand, listening and connecting are essential traits that were picked up during the interview process, particularly the in-person interview.

BEYOND IMPROV TO CONNECTING IN THE INTERVIEW

These improv games are a unique way to rewire our listening and connecting skills. They are fun and conducted in a safe space. In improv, the goal is to be funny, so making a fool of oneself is all part of the goal. It allows us to really stretch ourselves to act, speak, and behave in a way that is all welcomed. Through our ability to listen well we can demonstrate our ability to connect and voice how we are able to help them, the potential employer, resolve issues.

We are nearing the end of our process together! Next we'll discuss how you can leave a lasting impression that will have them excited about you and how you can make a difference at their organization.

CHAPTER 8

How to Leave a Lasting Impression

Be so good they can't ignore you.
– STEVE MARTIN

I frequently hear from a hiring leader something like, "I don't know, he didn't close me." The candidate didn't close the interview with an exclamation point. Instead, he left with a question mark.

You've prepared so well throughout the entire process and want to leave the interview with the best impression. This chapter draws upon things which we've talked about in previous chapters make a favorable impression.

HOW TO END WITH AN EXCLAMATION POINT

Imagine this scene. You're meeting with the CEO at the end of a long day of being interviewed. He is the ultimate decision maker and although it would have been great to meet him at the start when you were fresh, from the CEO's perspective, he wanted his entire team to meet you first so that he could gather their thoughts before meeting with you himself.

The meeting goes very well and you can see that you have connected with him. The interview has turned into more of a conversation and you're starting to discuss how—together—you can tackle some of the biggest issues facing the company. The meeting goes to 1.5 hours, well beyond the 1-hour mark that was originally set aside for the conversation, and now the meeting is ending.

One Way to End

"It was great to meet you," says that CEO. "I'm sure our CHRO will get in contact with you regarding next steps."

This is the time when you should make a final statement that is the exclamation point. What you say at this point in the process will leave an impression—whether positive or neutral or negative—in the mind of the CEO.

You could return the sentiment: "It was a pleasure. I enjoyed meeting everyone as well and look forward to the next steps." Or, you could be saying something like this:

A Powerful Ending

"Yes, I agree. It's been an incredible day here. I would like to leave you with this one point: 20 years ago when I started on my career journey, I could never have imagined that I'd be here in this spot. As a staffing specialist at a local savings and loan testing and interviewing tellers, I had no idea where my career would've taken me. The places I've travelled to find top talent for my companies, the partnerships developed to uncover the best talent in places that traditional recruiting would never unearth, to sitting here, being considered for the top Talent Acquisition spot for a global company, I can see how all along the way each role has been a stepping stone. I can see, from my day here and the challenges we discussed, all my experience and personal willpower to innovate and do things that are not typically done in the industry will all culminate to a very successful time here. Together we can build talent, strength, and capabilities that will take this organization to the next level and well into the future. Thank you for today, and I look forward to the next steps."

You stand, shake his hand, and together walk out of the office. Exclamation point!

NOW IT IS YOUR TURN

Let us create this story for you, the final story in your arsenal of stories so that you leave that meeting in the very best light.

This story draws from your "Tell me about yourself" story, mostly regarding your career steps up to the present moment. This connection with your early career steps communicates your passion for the line of work. For example, Daniel's story of becoming a police officer when he first graduated from college may seem like a far cry from his career goal of becoming an Executive Director for a community non-profit. Yet becoming a police officer because he wants to serve the community is perfectly in alignment with where he is today.

This story also pulls from your story about why you believe you are perfect for the role. Sure, you may not have exactly the requirements they are seeking; however, your history, experience, and passion for the work is in complete alignment. And you connected very well with everyone in the process, especially the hiring leader. It will seem like serendipity. That they are the luckiest company in the world because you are interested in their role. Not only interested, but see it as exactly where you need to be.

USE THE SAME PROCESS TO CRAFT YOUR FINAL STORY

As before in Chapter 4, write out your answer to the below questions long-hand. And as before, read it aloud and time yourself. Edit your answer to be around 60 seconds. Practice it in front of a mirror using body control and voice control while wearing the skin of your archetype. Practice at least 30 times. Get it down so that you come across exactly as you intend.

- What about the beginning and middle of your career path connects to today?
- What about the role plays directly to your strengths?

- What about the company is in alignment with your values?
- What contributions can you make to the company?
- What problems can you solve for the company?
- What about the role excited you?

This is not the time to say, "Well, I don't really have this or that in my background." They know how you don't quite meet the qualifications. It is a time to talk about the positives of what you can contribute. And that these positives will overshadow any little miss in experience.

Daniel's Closing Story

"Before I leave, I'd like to say that it has been a very exciting few days with you and your team. When I look back at my days as a police officer in New York, all I knew was that I wanted to serve my community. Walking the streets, talking with truant youth, listening to their stories, I would've never thought that I'd be here sitting with you, discussing the role of Executive Director for the Youth Association. I see that everything I've done in my past has been around community building. Even as a rabbi working across religious lines with leaders in different religions, we worked to respond to increasing hate crimes and create programs together. We were city council members, leaders of religious groups, and other community nonprofits. I can take the youth programs here at this organization to the next level. I am excited at the thought of working with you, the staff, and the many passionate volunteers to help this organization make a strong difference in the community and beyond. Whatever you decide I know will be the best decision for you and the organization. I am grateful for the opportunity, and encouraged that this organization is here helping the youth of the community."

Bam. Mic drop.

You've left the office feeling on top of the world! You've called me or your career coach and said, "I've nailed it!" You've sent thank you letters and two weeks have gone by. Now what? I recommend you move on. This is a really difficult thing to do for many people. You've poured your heart and soul into an opportunity and I am now asking you to move on to another opportunity. You've already imagined yourself on your first day at the job. And I'm suggesting you put your dreams aside and continue looking for other opportunities.

Like improv, it is helpful to live in the moment. Traveling in your time machine into the future is fun–buying your new briefcase for your new job–but, staying too long in that life may not serve you today in your job search. You are in a sales process that is fed by the number of applications submitted, or people networked with. Ride the emotional high by getting right back into looking for and applying to different opportunities.

Similarly, staying too long in the past–*oh, I should've said that instead*–is not the best place in time to linger. Perhaps that opportunity, that interview you just nailed, isn't really The One. Maybe The One is just around the corner. Pelé, considered one of the best soccer players of all time, once said, "Everything is practice." Gold medal game? Practice. World cup finals game? Practice. It's the same play for you.

Every interview is practice. You are getting better with each conversation. Gaining greater grit with each "no." These skills will continue to serve you well during your job search and beyond.

You've left an impression and continued to build your pipeline of potential companies that may one day be graced by your amazing talent. You're racing towards the finish line and feel a pop in your knee. You hobble to the side and sit down for a bit, but you're afraid that if you don't keep moving you may never finish the race. What do you do then? Finding a job you love, like finding the love of your life, is a little bit of luck (the ideal job opens right when you are searching) and a lot of endurance. It is a constant barrage of "thank you so much, but..." and deafening silence. The next chapter is for you when you start to feel that knee give out. When you start to lose steam. Hit that wall. And need to dig deep to finish the job.

CHAPTER 9

When (Not If) Things Get Hard

The beauty is that through disappointment you can gain clarity, and with clarity comes conviction and true originality.

– CONAN O'BRIEN

Successful people are survivors. We understand the meaning of grit. We've stayed the extra time, pushed through when others have dropped out. It is this determination that sets us apart. We know that often it is our determination that is the edge that helps us accomplish great things. We'd think that the search process is very much the same; however, there is a distinct difference. In the workplace we are in (or just left), people listened to us, deferred to our thoughts, and supported our vision. While searching for a job, we are facing multiple closed doors in the form of people and organizations that aren't interested in us. In the job search process, we will face rejection many more times than what we are used to. It is the nature of the process, and it can get to you.

"I don't know, I feel like I need to take a break from all of this," said Rakesh. "How can so many companies not see what I can contribute to their work teams?"

I agree with Rakesh because, being a member of Team Rakesh, I got to know him and his talents and began to think the same thing. How can they not see him? The job search is tiring. You're going to kiss a lot of frogs before you find your prince. You will be faced with a lot of possible prospects and for one reason or another you or they won't be interested. And there will be times when you just need to disconnect from all of it and focus on yourself. When you begin to get discouraged—and you probably will due to the nature of the process—I would like to pass along a few tips to help you through the rough patches.

WELCOME THE CLARITY

"This is my seventh rejection in a row," cried Kathy. "I'm not sure what I'm doing wrong."

How many times in our lives have we experienced seven rejections in a row? Perhaps sales executives are much more used to this than others. However, looking back, there aren't many periods of time in my career when I've experienced seven rejections in a period of a month. However, in the job search process, this is typical. Although difficult to consider, welcome the clarity.

Let's take this back to the dating analogy. Imagine you are dating a person and you are really into them, but they're secretly not as attracted to you. Would you rather they fake it and continue to go out with you, or would you rather know early on that they aren't into you so that you can end that relationship and focus on others? Most people would rather know.

A Recruiter's Perspective of Why

For whatever reason, the company has decided to focus on other candidates. Being an executive recruiter, I'll present you with a few reasons why we've decided on other candidates:

1. We found someone else that is a better fit for our needs.

2. They don't have another candidate, but do not think you'd be a great fit for their world due to _____ (insert one of many answers, like, the boss is extremely egotistical and can't stand the fact that you're a strong leader, the boss is extremely wimpy and is afraid you'll show him up, a colleague is threatened by you and sabotaged the situation, you're too strong for them in general, they really wanted someone with a different background, they really wanted someone with a higher degree, they really wanted someone from a competitor, etc.).

3. We put a freeze on hiring in general due to _____ (insert one of many business reasons from financial, restructuring, new leader with new ideas, etc.).

4. Someone suitable inside the company popped up at the last minute.

5. The hiring leader really had his heart set on hiring someone he's worked with in the past and you were in the mix as a comparison to that person.

6. The hiring manager wants to meet financials and knows that if she can keep the position unfilled for nine more months, she'll be closer to meeting financial goals.

7. The hiring manager wants to find the perfect person that meets every single requirement and is willing to wait a year until she finds the person.

8. The last time they hired someone from your (insert your alma mater, previous company, current industry here) it was a disaster, so they are afraid and willing to go with another candidate out of fear.

9. The hiring leader wants to retire within two years and she thinks that it will take much longer for you to be ready to be her successor, so she passes.

10. They aren't sure, but have a gut feeling it will not work out.

Bottom line, you may never know why they've decided to focus on other candidates. And it doesn't really matter, because if they were to hire you despite the fear, it wouldn't set you up in the best way. For example, if they hired you even though (taking reason 2) that boss is very egotistical and finds you a threat to his position, that would not be a great place for you to be. It wouldn't set you up for success as he would not be a strong supporter of you and may even sabotage your performance. I've talked with many executives that have started in companies where it was apparent early on that their boss was not and would never be a strong supporter of them. Despite that, they must try to navigate through that landmine and find a way to exit the role or, more drastically, the company.

The clarity of being rejected from a role is a good thing, because you don't want to be somewhere they cannot handle the real you. And I strongly believe that not everyone would be a great fit at every company.

How Clarity Helped Julie Move on to Great Things

Julie was a marketing and communications leader. She came to me to share that she felt like her boss may be pushing her out of the company. She had been feeling signals for a few months, and then her boss mentioned something that made it very clear that Julie's days are numbered. Having worked with Julie in the past, I knew her more than a typical client, and all my experiences with her have been exceptional. She did everything she said she would in a very timely manner and provided excellent innovative ideas to get messages across. In all regards, I've always thought of Julie as a star performer. However, because of the negative energy from her boss, over time Julie started to wonder if she was doing something wrong. It was at that point that I encouraged her to find another job. It was time for her to stop listening to the negative voice in her head, and to remember that she is a talented and amazing marketing and communication leader. Julie floated her résumé and landed a fantastic job executing incredible communication programs where she reported directly to the CEO. Within a year, they promoted her, and today she is earning significantly more than if she had stayed at the other company. All the lies that her little negative voice was telling her evaporated. Julie realized that there wasn't anything lacking. She was enough. And in fact, more than enough for her next employer.

QUIET YOUR AMYGDALA: IT MAKES THINGS TOO UNCLEAR

Your amygdala is very active when you are in the middle of a job search process. If you've hit a funk, check in with your amygdala to see if it has been busy sowing seeds of doubt. Some people have physical manifestations when their amygdala is working overtime. I click my teeth together when I start down a negative talk spin. I've known people who tap their fingers or shake their leg. Often just recognizing that the amygdala is working overdrive stops the negative chatter.

Here are a few examples of how one executive quieted their amygdala.

Meet Vicky: How She Quieted Her Amygdala

Vicki, a long-time successful executive for a large international firm was very happy with her life. However, deep in her heart she yearned to work for a start-up, taking an organization from its earliest state to exponential growth. She sent her résumé to several of these firms. But again and again, she stopped the interview process midway for different reasons—they aren't stable, they don't have medical insurance, they won't pay me enough—all without finishing the process to see if they could offer her what she wants. Soon she became aware of her self-sabotaging decisions and made a commitment to herself to ride the job search process all the way through to the end until she received an offer. Today, she works for a well-funded start-up firm working her magic and helping the company grow by leaps and bounds.

If your amygdala is holding you back by telling you lies to keep you safe and small, it is time to demote it. Rewrite its job description from Chief Safety Officer to Safety Assistant. Just tell it to let you know that something may be a danger and leave the rest to you. Thank you very much.

HONOR THE CONNECTIONS

Living in the moment of improv, you do not know what the future holds. And you do not know how what was just said will shape what you do in a few moments. Similarly, in the job search process, you never know how the people you've talked with today can shape tomorrow.

It's a Small World

Cindy once interviewed for a Vice President of HR position for a nationwide transportation company. Cindy didn't end up getting the job. A year had passed when she came across a résumé with a very familiar company and realized that it was the incumbent of the transportation company. This woman was applying for a position at her company. In full disclosure, Cindy told this person that she actually applied for her job at the transportation company. The woman replied and said, "Wow, be glad you didn't get the position. It was a really tough work environment there." Back then, Cindy was heartbroken that she didn't get the position, but now she's glad. Today Cindy and that individual are part of the same mastermind circle. Sometimes, even if you don't get the position, you'll end up making connections that become important contacts in the future.

In the interview process, you may not know the reasons for the reactions people have. It is easy to fill in the blanks or the silence with a story. The amygdala will attempt to fill it with a story, and most likely it isn't a positive reason.

Our amygdala tends to give us the bleakest of reasons. If you are fortunate to receive direct feedback from an interview, I recommend you take it with both gratitude and a grain of salt. Gratitude, because many organizations will not go to the extent of providing feedback to rejected candidates. They are more concerned with a possibility of a lawsuit than in taking the time to provide honest feedback. A grain of salt, because oftentimes their perceptions of you are more a reflection of them than of you.

Yes, I am absolutely convinced that when you look in your toolbox of tricks, you'll find that you have persevered through very difficult things in your past and have showed a tremendous amount of grit. With this determination, you've emerged very successful. It is the same for the job search process. You're not alone in this regard. Every job seeker that I work with shares how demotivating it is. I've heard that when job seekers accept the clarity of a rejection and honor the people they've met along the way, it helps them dig deep and continue forward.

You are successful. You are motivated. Your hard work will pay off, and you'll land the job that you will love. The job that will be meaningful and make a difference in this world.

CHAPTER 10

Yes, And! What's Next?

Find out who you are and be that person. That's what
your soul was put on this Earth to be. Find that truth,
live that truth, and everything else will come.
— ELLEN DEGENERES

At some point in our career we come to a juncture. We are faced with accepting a position where we will continue our path of climbing the corporate ladder and earning a solid income for our family. Or possibly taking a turn down a path that gives a little back.

I've seen this pivot in many job seekers and in myself. The desire to do something meaningful grows. The aspiration to make a difference in this world spreads. This pivot at first feels too big, too scary. Like standing on the edge of a cliff and looking down to a pool of sparkling blue water. And you want to jump.

Darlene leaving an insurance firm to join a nature preservation organization. Alex leaving his family's business to help employees manage through large-scale change. Vince leaving his Chief Medical Officer role to work with organizations creating greater access to healthcare. And me leaving my corporate human resources job to become a career coach to help people find jobs they love. The pivot appears scary, at first. Yet once you make the change, it feels like you are doing what you are meant to do in this world.

The job search process has changed over the years. Articulating the desire for this pivot to employers has changed as well. It relies much more on technology and requires us to be ready at the quick with our compelling stories. Because we've had so many years of success, our tendency is to ad lib off the top of our heads. We turn to the experts at improv, comedians, to practice tools that make them great. In a safe environment where laughing at one's self is the norm, we rehearse our compelling stories–that are rooted in truth. Through this process we find a stronger voice, a more authentic powerful voice, our voice.

My hope is that through this unconventional process you've gained a new skill that you can use beyond the job search process. When you are planning your first 90 days on the job, your powerful authentic voice is used to set the plan forward. You have moved beyond the first stories that every candidate needs to have in their toolbox. You have a methodology with which to continue crafting compelling stories that captivate and motivate your teams, investors, and clients. You are a master at listening, connecting, and living in the moment.

Perhaps you'll even introduce some of these games to your team. Games like "yes, and" or "change three things." So that everyone within your team practices in the safe space of improv to stretch and grow.

I'm excited to hear how these techniques have helped you prepare for the age-old situation of the job search. I would love to hear your stories of self-discovery, your challenges, and your successes. Please stay in contact. I'd love to hear when you've landed a job of your dreams, a job that you love. One that gives you a tremendous amount of meaning and purpose. Connect with me and drop me a line.

Brilliant Sayings That Came out of Someone Else's Mouth

I must start with a list of brilliant quotes from some of the funniest people of all time. Some quotes didn't make it to the previous chapters. Some quotes are from controversial comedians. If you may be offended by that, please don't read on. I've loved each one of these comedians over the years and have laughed so hard at their comedy. I truly value their gift to the world.

Love yourself first and everything else falls into line. You really have to love yourself to get anything done in this world.
— LUCILLE BALL

Be easy on yourself. Have fun. Only hang around people that are positive and make you feel good. Anybody who doesn't make you feel good, kick them to the curb. And the earlier you start in your life, the better.
— AMY POEHLER

*Do It Under The Influence of Yourself! That's what we're
shooting for! Get drunk and make your dreams come true!*
— AZIZ ANSARI

Work hard, be kind, and amazing things will happen.
— CONAN O'BRIEN

*Take your risks now, as you grow older you become more
fearful and less flexible. And I mean that literally. I hurt my
knee this week on the treadmill, and it wasn't even on.*
— AMY POEHLER

*Every great thing starts with an idea, followed by
a doubt and finally a resolve to abandon or pursue.
Victory is a treacherous journey.*
— DANE COOK

*If you feel rooted in your home and family, if you're
active in your community, there's nothing more
empowering. The best way to make a difference in the
world is to start by making a difference in your own life.*
— JULIA LOUIS-DREYFUS

*The best piece of advice someone has ever given me was
'do it scared.' And no matter if you're scared, just go
ahead and do it anyway because you might as well do
it scared, so it will get done and you will feel so much
better if you step out of your comfort zone.*
— SHERRI SHEPHERD

Laugh loudly, laugh often, and most importantly, laugh at yourself.
— CHELSEA HANDLER

I urge you all today, especially today during these times of chaos and war, to love yourself without reservations and to love each other without restraint.
— MARGARET CHO

I'm here today because I refused to be unhappy. I took a chance.
— WANDA SYKES

Love what you do. Get good at it. Competence is a rare commodity in this day and age. And let the chips fall where they may.
— JON STEWART

You can only really learn from failure ... to win you need to fail, and fail hard.
— AISHA TYLER

People may hate you for being different and not living by society's standards, but deep down they wish they had the courage to do the same.
— KEN HART

You're only given a little spark of madness. You mustn't lose it.
— ROBIN WILLIAMS

*You just be honest about who you are, and if you don't
end up with any friends, then good for you.*
— CHELSEA HANDLER

*You can't be that kid standing at the top of the water
slide overthinking it. You have to go down the chute.*
— TINY FEY

*In order to succeed, your desire for success should be
greater than your fear of failure.*
— BILL COSBY

Always do whatever's next.
— GEORGE CARLIN

*I think the difference between being miserable and
finding happiness is just a matter of perspective. If you
live your life defining yourself by what other people
think of you, it's a form of self-torture.*
— SARAH SILVERMAN

*I went to a bookstore and asked the saleswoman,
'Where's the self-help section?' She said if she told me, it
would defeat the purpose.*
— GEORGE CARLIN

Don't sweat the petty things and don't pet the sweaty things.
— GEORGE CARLIN

As you navigate through the rest of your life, be open to collaboration. Other people and other people's ideas are often better than your own. Find a group of people who challenge and inspire you, spend a lot of time with them, and it will change your life.
— AMY POEHLER

Brilliant Books Written by Other People

This was the most influential book of my life. This book opened my ears to the trash-talk I was telling myself. I was introduced to my amygdala–the annoying, yet potentially helpful part of my brain. Eckhart Tolle's book, *The Power of Now*. It wasn't an easy read for me, but I couldn't put it down.

Brian Tracy, is a motivator of so many things. I call him the Guru of Getting Things Done. I love his book, *Eat That Frog!: 21 Great Ways to Stop Procrastinating and Get More Done in Less Time.* Whenever I get stuck, I pick up that frog and eat it! And if there are two, I eat the ugliest one first. You can also find a wealth of information on his website www.briantracy.com

I love Amy Van Court's book, *Escaping Career Prison: Three Keys to Breaking Free and Finding Work You Love.* She has helped so many people open the cage of their career prison. In many ways, this book is a continuation of hers. You can find Amy at www.possibilitiesunlimited.org.

For those of you suffering from what I call Career Post-Traumatic Stress, Mary Hayes Grieco's book, *Unconditional Forgiveness,* is a must. She shares steps that can be the elixir that dissolves a bad working situation from your life.

ACKNOWLEDGMENTS

If the thought of standing on stage is frightening, don't tell people you are writing a book. The amount of criticism and "helpful" hints that are offered is enough to make you question your sanity. Putting out your work, your deepest thoughts, is like opening the kimono in front of thousands of people. But I *had to* write this book. I had to get these ideas out. It was more than determination, it was a compulsion. When I finished the first manuscript in the quiet of my sister's home at the very top of a mountain on O'ahu, I was overcome with a deep sense of peace. It was almost enough just to get it all down on paper. Thank you, Joan, Tracy, Nolan, and Bella, for allowing me full run of your peaceful home to jam my 80's music and write.

The single most instrumental person who helped me—without her tough love, expertise, and support it would've taken me longer, cost more money, and been all around more painful to do—is my publisher, Angela Lauria. I knew from the moment I first talked with you that you were my kind of peep. Your honest, authentic approach is like a nudge at exactly the right time. Thank you for calling me out and challenging me to dig deep.

To the Morgan James Publishing team: Special thanks to David Hancock, CEO & Founder for believing in me and my message. To my Author Relations Manager, Aubrey Kosa, thanks for making the process seamless and easy. Many more thanks to everyone else, but especially Jim Howard, Bethany Marshall, and Nickcole Watkins.

To Mary Stultz, the most extraordinary, joyful coach I've come across (and I've talked with many). I love and adore you to pieces. You've been through it all with me from my days of leaving corporate America to today. Thank you for being perfectly you.

A few months before I wrote this book, I co-authored a book with Brian Tracy, entrepreneur, professional speaker, international best-selling author, and CEO of Brian Tracy International. That experience broke the seal. It was immediately after I wrote that chapter that I knew I could write my own book. Thank you for being in my life for many years from your Phoenix Seminar from the Psychology of Achievement, to your *How to Write a Book* series, to inviting me to co-author a book with you. Thank you for helping hundreds, thousands, and probably millions of people achieve great things.

My first year at Vanderbilt's MBA program, I was horrified when I got back my first paper. It was covered in red ink as if you had dipped the entire page in a vat of red. I knew my writing skills weren't fantastic, but I didn't realize how bad. I immediately went to a bookstore and bought Strunk &

White's book *Elements of Style* and began writing and writing and writing more. Over the school year, papers came back with less and less red ink. If it weren't for your red ball point pen, Bruce, if you had not taken the time to painstakingly edit, I might not have become a writer. Thank you, Dr. Bruce Barry, Brownlee O. Currey, Jr., Professor of Management, Organization Studies, Ethics, and Social Responsibility at the Owen School of Management at Vanderbilt University. Thank you for caring for this one student.

On a hunch, I attended the Berkeley Improv class. I did it wondering: *Could we teach people confidence and charisma in interviews using improv techniques?* This hunch turned into hours of coaching for job seekers–especially introverts or closet extroverts–and became major sections of this book. Since my clumsy first attempts at Berkeley Improv, I've attended improv classes at the Pan Theater in Oakland, watched countless "Whose Line Is It Anyway?" clips, and become a student in Steve Martin's Masterclass on comedy. Thank you to all my teachers, facilitators, and fellow participants. Thank you for the space to fail and laugh at ourselves.

Thank you, Amy Van Court, author of *Escaping Career Prison: Three Keys to Breaking Free and Finding Work You Love*. From the day I read your book in September 2013, I've recommended it to countless others. Thank you for remembering my email to you many years ago when I mentioned to you that I wanted to write a book. I am glad to be a comrade with you in helping people find meaningful work.

To my constant daily companion, Alexa. Without which I couldn't demand streaming 80s music, which I've found is my preferred background sound while writing. (What a world we live in that we thank our bots.)

To my best friend and husband, Edgar, I thank you for countless hours of listening to and encouraging me–holding your tongue while allowing me to stream forth idea after idea. You are my #1 cheerleader. The person who thinks the best of me, wants the best for me, and lets me try countless crazy ideas. Remember the many ideas I've had over the years? Not once did you poo-poo on an idea. How do you do that? Thank you so much. I'm so grateful that we met long ago at Vanderbilt University's MBA program in Nashville. Thank you for hotly pursuing me our entire first year even though I wasn't looking for love (that's my story and I'm sticking to it).

And to my two boys, Eric and Andrew, thank you for being my source of inspiration. If it weren't for the pending college tuition, I'd be sitting on the couch watching another TV marathon. To Eric, your adventurous spirit and kind heart and Andrew, your sharp wit and sweet soul, I love you both so much.

ABOUT THE AUTHOR

For the past 20 years, Cara has helped people get jobs. Before, as a corporate recruiter and headhunter for large national and international companies—ARAMARK, Kaiser Permanente®, Baxter Healthcare—and small- to mid-sized firms from Silicon Valley start-ups to staffing agencies where she has found and wooed candidates for hard-to-fill  C-suite and physician positions. Now, she helps people get jobs while sitting on the other side of the negotiating table as a career coach, sharing what goes on behind the curtain of corporate human resources staffing.

Cara is CEO of Ready Reset Go™, a career coaching firm that helps people figure out why it's taking so long to land a job. The more successful you are and the longer you've been working, the harder it is for you to get a job. If you are a star performer, awesome is oh-so-normal for you. And if you've been working for a while, you can do a lot of things.

The problem with being able to do a lot of things is that Recruiters want to fit candidates in a box. Cara works with clients to avoid niche-phobia and articulate their incredible talents and achievements using innovative methods.

Cara is a recognized expert, speaker, and trainer, and has taught on today's job search methods, uncovering unconscious biases, giving and getting feedback, recruiting search techniques, and improv interviewing preparation. In addition to publishing this book, Cara is co-authoring a book, *Ready Set Go!*, with world-renowned International Best Selling author and business consultant, Brian Tracy.

Cara has a MBA from Vanderbilt University and a Bachelor of Business from the University of Hawaii at Manoa. She is a certified Senior Professional Human Resources, a Certified Professional Résumé Writer, a Certified Professional Career Coach, and member of the Forbes Coaches Council. She is also Lominger Recruiting Architect® and TRACOM® Group Social Styles certified. She is on the Board of Directors of Wardrobe for Opportunity, a nonprofit in Oakland ending poverty by helping people get a job, keep a job, and build a career.

Cara resides in the San Francisco Bay Area with her husband and two sons, where she runs throughout the East Bay hills training for marathons and crazy fun 24-hour relay races.

Cara loves to hear from people, so feel free to connect:
www.linkedin.com/in/caraheilmann/
www.readyresetgo.com
@CaraHeilmann

THANK YOU

Thank you for reading my book! There are so many things that I wanted to talk about but couldn't fit it all in. It has been an amazing journey to write this book, and I feel like you've been on this journey with me. Now that you have tools to help you use your powerful voice in the job search process, I have a free gift for you to help you land the job of your dreams.

My assessment, **Where the Heck Are My Job Offers?** can help you diagnose exactly what's going wrong in your job search. Job seekers ask me to help them diagnose why they haven't received job offers. Together we figure out exactly where they are tripping up and exactly what they need to do to fix it. This quick assessment is the first part of that diagnosis, and is yours free as my gift to you.

To take this assessment, go to my website at https://www.readyresetgo.com/ireadyourbook.

If you have any questions, I love to hear from readers. Send me a comment from my page at www.readyresetgo.com.

Let's do this!

Cara

Morgan James
Speakers Group

www.TheMorganJamesSpeakersGroup.com

We connect Morgan James published authors with live and online events and audiences who will benefit from their expertise.